TENSES ARE MY TEACHER

HINDI TO ENGLISH

PRACTICE CONTINUOUS TENSES

PRACTICE BOOK

Published On September 4, 2024

AMRITASHAAN

Name

Address

Message

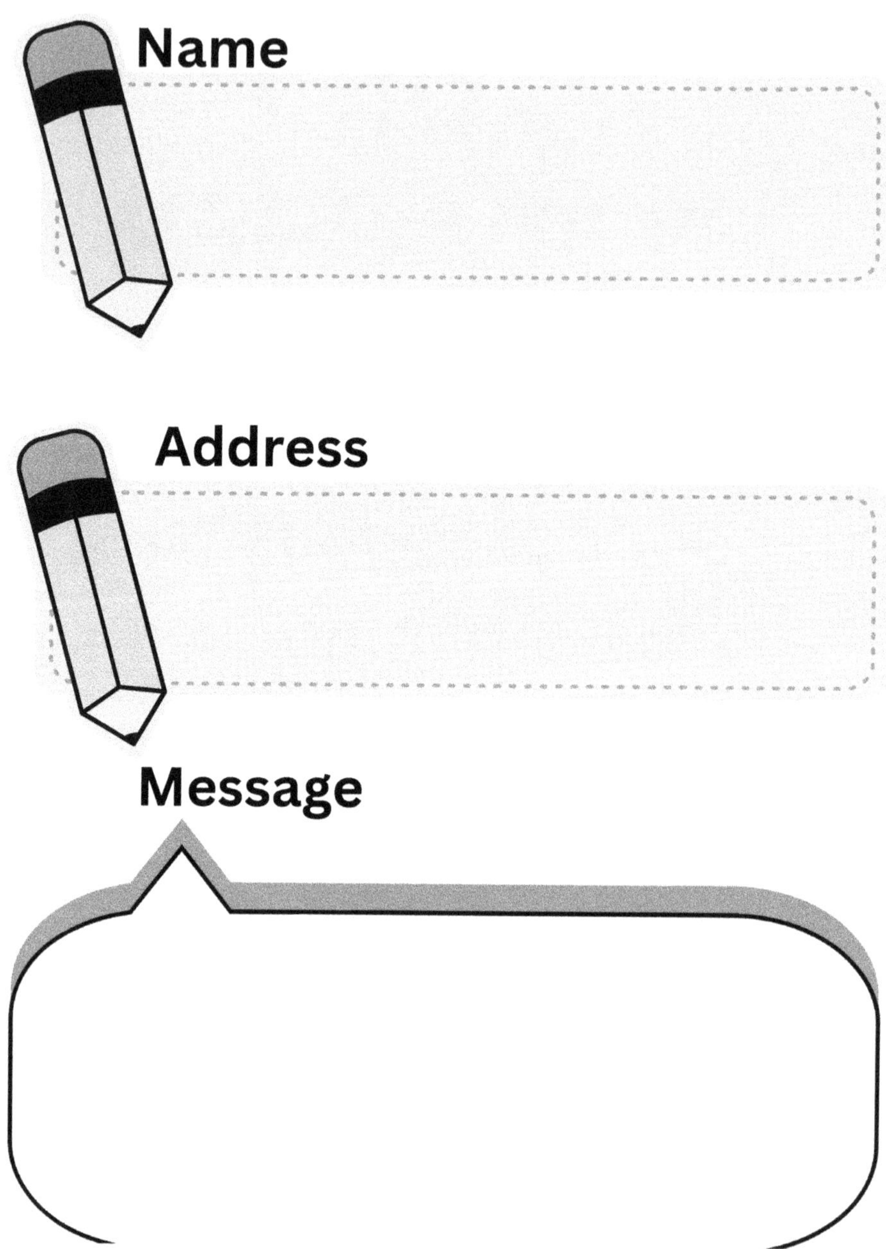

English Speaking

A Practice Book For English Learners

AMRITASHAAN | PRACTICE ALL CONTINUOUS | 3

Practice book

FOR

Present Continuous

Past Continuous

Future Continuous

By : **AMRITASHAAN**

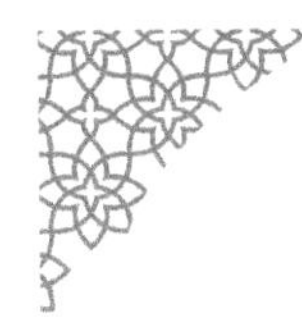

MY FAMILY

Life is a voyage made possible by the care you give! The entire My Book series pays gratitude to family, and may the spirits be filled with bliss for all.

With Loving Blessings
For
My Nephew
On
His Birthday
September 5

Welcome Learners !

It is delightful to see that you are at Vol. 4 and are improving your language proficiency. Through straightforward and highly effective practices, you'll further gain confidence in your English speaking abilities. Engaging in these exercises will not only familiarize you with the 'is, am, are, was, were, will be, shall be + first form of Verb + ing but also enhance your ability to use the correct verbs while conversing in English. Embrace the power of tense as your guide, turning it into your teacher to facilitate effective communication in English.

TABLE OF CONTENTS

TABLE OF CONTENTS

TABLE OF CONTENTS

TENSES ARE MY TEACHER - Vol. 4
Practice Continuous Tenses

Copyright Office Government Of India
Dated : 28/10/2024
L-156062/2024

This self-published book has undergone thorough efforts by the author to ensure the accuracy of its content. Unauthorized usage or reproduction of any part of this book is strictly prohibited without the author's written consent.

The primary goal of this book is to offer learners valuable self-practice material for self-improvement.

Disclaimer: The author has crafted this book based on personal experiences and original ideas. All materials presented are innovative practice resources. It is important to note that this book does not adhere to any prescribed syllabus, although it is highly beneficial for English language learners seeking effective self-practice materials.

About The Author

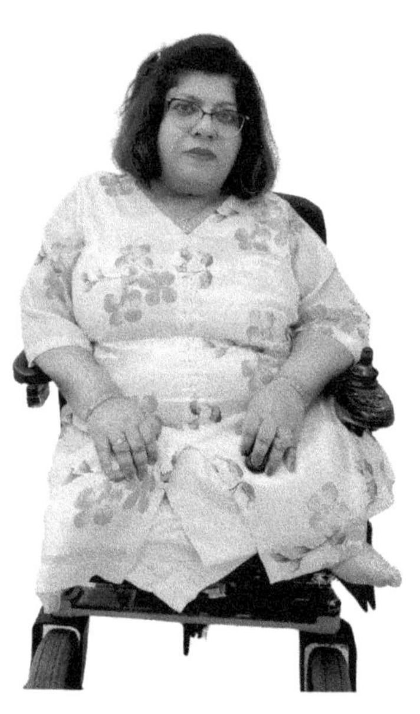

Amritashaan is a distinguished author and motivational speaker with a profound expertise in English language education. Her innovative teaching methods have revolutionized the way countless learners approach the language, significantly enhancing the skills of both native and non-native speakers. With a remarkable collection of books on mastering English, Amritashaan has solidified her reputation as a leading IELTS trainer, making substantial contributions to the field of language education. Her YouTube channel, website serve as a valuable resource, offering insightful guidance and motivation to learners. Whether through her meticulously crafted books or comprehensive practice materials, engaging with her work guarantees an extraordinary and transformative learning experience. In her hometown, she is celebrated as an exceptional educator, admired for her unwavering dedication to the advancement of language teaching.

OBJECTIVE

English has emerged as the primary means of communication for millions of people worldwide. It is employed daily to interact with friends, colleagues, and more. To actively participate in this global discourse, familiarity with English, including a grasp of its various tenses, is essential. The purpose of crafting this book is to:

- Foster a comprehensive understanding of the practical applications of English tenses.
- Facilitate independent practice for learners.
- Supply impactful materials for tangible improvement.
- Enhance proficiency in Hindi-English oral translation for effective English speaking.
- Enable native learners to converse fluently in English.

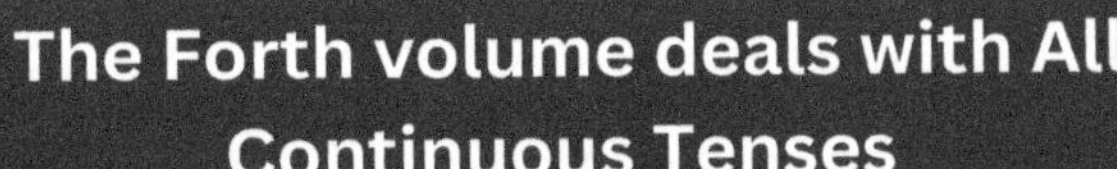

PRACTICE WAY

- Tense के नियमों को ध्यान से पढ़ें।
- याद रखें कि आप जिस क्रिया को अभ्यास कर रहे हैं, वह मौलिक क्रिया होनी चाहिए।
- हिंदी पाठ को धीरे-धीरे पढ़ें।
- धीरे-धीरे क्रियाओं को सोचें।
- अब हिंदी संस्करण खोलें और पूरे पाठ का अनुवाद करने का प्रयास करें।
- दिए गए क्रियाओं की मदद लें।
- इसे मौखिक रूप से करें।
- अगले पृष्ठ पर अपने काम की जाँच करें।
- नियमित रूप से अभ्यास करें और आत्म-विश्वास से बोलें।

- Read the rules of Tense carefully.
- Remember the base verb you are going to practice.
- Read Hindi passage slowly.
- Think of verbs by and by.
- Now keep open Hindi version and try to translate the whole passage in English.
- Take help of given verbs.
- Do it orally.
- Check your work at next page.
- Practice and speak confidently.

UNDERSTAND PRESENT CONTINUOUS

प्रेजेंट कंटीन्यूस टेंस (**Present Continuous Tense**) का प्रयोग हिंदी में किसी कार्य के वर्तमान में जारी रहने को दर्शाने के लिए किया जाता है।
जैसे कि:

- मैं खाना खा रहा हूँ। (I am eating food.)
- तुम किताब पढ़ रहे हो। (You are reading a book.)
- वह चित्र बना रही है। (She is drawing.)
- मेरी बहन टीवी देख रही है। (My sister is watching TV.)
- बच्चे बगीचे में खेल रहे हैं। (Children are playing in the garden.)
- हम खाना बना रहे हैं। (We are cooking.)
- सूरज चमक रहा है। (The sun is shining.)
- पक्षी गा रहे हैं। (The birds are singing.)
- हमारे प्रिंसिपल भाषण दे रहे हैं। (Our principal is giving a speech.)
- भगवान हमें देख रहे हैं। (God is watching us.)

Rule in HINDI

यह वाक्य बोलना या लिखना बहुत आसान है। जब कोई क्रिया वर्तमान समय में जारी होती है, तो हमें 'is', 'am', 'are' का प्रयोग करना होता है, जिसमें क्रिया के मूल रूप के साथ '-ing' जोड़ा जाता है। 'Is' का प्रयोग एकवचन कर्ता के साथ होता है, 'Am' का प्रयोग 'I' के साथ होता है और 'Are' का प्रयोग बहुवचन कर्ता के साथ + 'You' के साथ होता है।

Positive Sentence Structure

Rule : is, am, are + 1stverb +ing

- मेरे शिक्षक हमें पढ़ा रहे हैं। (My teacher is teaching us.)
- मैं नाश्ता कर रहा हूँ। (I am having breakfast.)
- मैं गाना गा रही हूँ। (I am singing.)
- तुम दौड़ रहे हो। (You are running.)
- तुम किताब पढ़ रही हो। (You are reading a book.)
- मेरा मित्र गाड़ी चला रहा है। (My friend is driving a car.)
- वह पानी पी रहा है। (He is drinking water.)
- फूल खिल रहे हैं। (Flowers are blooming.)
- नदियाँ बह रही हैं। (The rivers are flowing.)

Rule in English

It is very easy to speak or write these sentences. When an action is ongoing in the present time, we need to use 'is', 'am', or 'are' with the base form of the verb + '-ing'. 'Is' is used with singular subjects, 'am' is used with 'I', and 'are' is used with plural subjects as well as with 'you'.

Positive Sentence Structure

Rule : is, am, are + 1stverb +ing

- I am traveling to Paris next summer.
- You are learning how to play the guitar someday.
- Children are growing up to become the leaders of tomorrow.
- My friend is starting his own business next year.
- We are all meeting again someday.
- English is becoming a global language one day.
- Books are helping people know their past.
- India is emerging as the strongest nation of the world.
- The planet Earth is going to retain its beauty and purity even in the future.

Rule in English

Negative Sentence Structure

Rule : is, am, are + not + 1st verb +ing

- She is not eating her dinner right now.
- They are not playing basketball at the moment.
- I am not studying for my exam this evening.
- He is not sleeping in his room at this time.
- We are not watching TV tonight.
- The dog is not barking loudly today.
- The children are not swimming in the pool right now.
- Mary and Tom are not arguing over the project.
- The birds are not chirping outside the window.
- It is not raining heavily this afternoon.
- I am reading this book to improve my tenses.

Interrogative Sentence Structure

Rule : is, am, are + Subject + 1st verb + ing + Object?

- Are you studying for your exam tomorrow?
- Is she working on the new project with her team?
- Are they playing soccer in the park right now?
- Are we having dinner at that new restaurant tonight?
- Is he watching a movie at home this evening?
- Are you listening to music while you clean your room?
- Are they waiting for the bus at the usual stop?
- Are you cooking dinner for your family tonight?
- Is she attending the conference next week?
- Are they discussing the budget in the meeting right now?
- What are you planning for coming weekend?
- Why are looking off colour today?

मैं जॉय हूँ, सात साल का बच्चा हूँ, और मैं यहाँ आपकी मदद के लिए हूँ ताकि आप अंग्रेजी बोलने का

अभ्यास कर सकें। मैंने सरल हिंदी में कुछ कहा है —शायद अपने बारे में या किसी अन्य विषय पर। आपका काम है इसे अंग्रेजी में बोलने की कोशिश करना। आपको पूरा अनुवाद धीरे-धीरे मिलेगा, लेकिन उसे देखने से पहले, ईमानदारी से अनुवाद करने और ज़ोर से बोलने का अभ्यास करें।

आपका ईमानदार प्रयास आपको सफलता दिलाएगा, और आपकी सफलता आपके दिल को खुशी से भर देगी और आपके मनोबल को ऊंचा उठाएगी!

I'm Joy, a seven-year-old kid, and I'm here to help you practice speaking English. I've said something in simple Hindi—maybe about myself or on different topics. Your job is to try to say it in English. You'll get the full translations eventually, but before you check them, make sure to practice translating and speaking out loud with focus and sincerity.

Your sincere effort will bring you success and your success will fill your heart with joy and uplift your spirit!

- मैं अपने दोस्त का **इंतजार कर रहा हूं** वह मुझे **लेने आ रहा है |** (waiting, coming)
- तुम यहाँ **बैठे हो** और तुम्हारी माँ घर पर तुम्हारा **इंतज़ार कर रही है |** (sitting, waiting)
- आप उसे सलाह दे रहे हैं क्योंकि वह अजीब तरीके से काम कर रहा है। (advising, doing)
- घड़ी तो समय पर चल रही है लेकिन मैं गति खो रहा हूँ। (running, losing)
- कई लोग गरीबी की समस्या से जूझ रहे हैं और कई लोग धन-संपदा से भरपूर हैं। (grappling, rolling)
- मैं कुछ वाक्यों का अंग्रेजी में अनुवाद कर रहा हूं और इससे मुझे अपनी अंग्रेजी सुधारने में मदद मिल रही है। (translating, helping)
- खरगोश तेजी से भाग रहा है लेकिन कछुआ धीरे चल रहा है | (running, moving)
- काले बादल छा रहे हैं और जल्द ही बारिश होने वाली है। (overcasting, going to rain)
- बाजीगर अपने करतब दिखा रहा है और बच्चे हंस-हंसकर लोटपोट हो रहे हैं। (showing, rolling in laughter)

- I **am waiting** for my friend, he **is coming** to pick me up.
- You **are sitting** here and your mother **is waiting** for you at home.
- You **are advising** him as he **is doing** the things strangely.
- The clock **is running** on time but i **am losing** the pace.
- Many people **are grappling** with the problem of poverty and many **are rolling** in wealth.
- I **am translating** some sentences into English and this **is helping** me improve my English.
- The rabbit **is running** fast but the tortoise **is moving** slowly.
- The dark clouds **are overcasting** the cloud and it **is going** to rain soon.
- The juggler **is showing** his tricks and the children **are rolling** in laughter.

Practice Time 2

- बच्चा कहानी की किताब नहीं पढ़ रहा है इसलिए वह अपने खाली समय का सही उपयोग नहीं कर रहा है। **(not reading, making)**
- मुझे नींद नहीं आ रही है मैं अपना काम ख़ुशी से कर रहा हूँ। **(not feeling, doing)**
- वह इस परियोजना में सहायता नहीं कर रही है क्योंकि वह इसके लिए योग्य नहीं है। **(not assisting, is not)**
- खिलाड़ी उत्कृष्टता के लिए प्रयास नहीं कर रहे हैं, वे अपने प्रशंसकों का विश्वास खो रहे हैं।**(not striving, losing trust)**
- जॉय सोफे पर नहीं सो रहा है। वह अपनी पढ़ाई की मेज पर ऊंघ रहा है। **(not snoozing, dozing)**
- मुझे किसी भी कठिनाई का सामना नहीं करना पड़ रहा है क्योंकि मैं इस कार्य के लिए तैयार हूं। **(not encountering, prepared)**
- डॉक्टर दस्तावेज को स्कैन नहीं कर रहे हैं क्योंकि मरीज पहले ही अंतिम सांस ले रहा है। **(scanning, breathing his last)**
- कप्तान टीम की कमान नहीं संभाल रहा है। वह अपने सदस्यों की रणनीतियों का निरीक्षण कर रहा है। **(is not commanding, observing)**

- The child **is not reading** a story book so he **is not making** good use of his free time.
- I **am not feeling** sleepy I **am doing** my work happily.
- She **is not assisting** with the project as she i**s not qualified** for the same.
- The players **are not striving** for excellence, they **are going to lose** the trust of their fans.
- Joy **is not snoozing** on the couch. He **is dozing** at his study table.
- I **am not encountering** any difficulties as i **am prepared** for the feat.
- The doctor **is not scanning** the document as the patient **is already breathing his last.**
- The captain **is not commanding** the team. He **is observing** the strategies of his members.

- क्या मेरे दोस्त सरप्राइज पार्टी की योजना बना रहे हैं? **(planning)**
- क्या रसोइया अभी डिनर तैयार कर रहा है? **(preparing)**
- क्या ड्राइवर आज हमेशा की तरह ही रास्ता अपना रहा है? **(taking)**
- क्या भगवान हम पर नज़र रख रहे हैं? **(watching over)**
- क्या बाहर बारिश हो रही है? **(raining)**
- क्या आज दोपहर मौसम सुधर रहा है? **(improving)**
- क्या इंजन अजीब सी आवाज़ कर रहा है? **(making a strange noise)**
- क्या ये किताबें लाइब्रेरी में वापस की जा रही हैं? **(are being returned)**
- क्या यात्री जल्द ही स्टेशन पर पहुँच रहे हैं? **(arriving at)**
- क्या गाड़ी सुचारू रूप से चल रही है? **(running smoothly)**
- कोने में आखिरी बेंच पर कौन बैठा है? **(sitting)**
- मेरी अनुपस्थिति में यहाँ क्या हो रहा है? **(going on)**
- आप अपनी छुट्टियों में कहाँ जा रहे हैं? **(going)**
- आप अपने नए बने घर में कब शिफ्ट हो रहे हैं? **(shifting)**

- Are my friends **planning** a surprise party?
- Is the cook **preparing** dinner right now?
- Is the driver **taking** the usual route today?
- Is God **watching** over us?
- Is it **raining** outside?
- Is the weather **improving** this afternoon?
- Is the engine **making** a strange noise?
- Are these books **being returned** to the library?
- Are the travelers **arriving** at the station soon?
- Is the car **running** smoothly?
- Who **is sitting** on the last bench in the corner?
- What **is going** on here in my absence?
- Where are you **going** in your holidays?
- When **are you shifting** to your newly constructed house?

- Present Continuous
- Make use of 'is, am, are + 1stv + ing
- Negative sentences take 'is, am, are, + not + 1stv + ing'
- Interrogative sentences take 'Is, Am, Are + subject + 1stv + ing + object?'

The present continuous tense describes actions that are currently happening or ongoing at the moment of speaking.

मैं अपनी अंग्रेजी सुधारने के लिए एक किताब खरीद रहा हूँ। यह किताब मुझे भाषा के बारे में बहुत सी बातें सीखने में मदद कर रही है। मेरे पिता कह रहे हैं कि किताबें ज्ञान का भंडार होती हैं। मैं रोजाना थोड़ा अभ्यास कर रहा हूँ और अभ्यास से मुझे आत्मविश्वास मिल रहा है। अंततः, मैं दूसरों के साथ अंग्रेजी में बातचीत करने में कभी संकोच नहीं कर रहा हूँ।

VERBS TO HELP
buying, helping, saying, training, feeling

I am buying a book to improve my English. This book is helping me learn a lot of things about language. My father is saying that books are a storehouse of knowledge. I am training myself a little bit daily and training is giving me confidence. Finally, I am not feeling hesitant to converse in English with others.

What three important things you are doing to take your English to next level?

आइए हम सामाजिक शिविर का नज़ारा देखें। बच्चे एक साथ कई तरह के खेल खेल रहे हैं। वे खेल के मैदान में दौड़ रहे हैं, हँस रहे हैं और खुशी से चिल्ला रहे हैं। कुछ बच्चे पेड़ों की छाँव में रंग-बिरंगे चित्र बना रहे हैं। दूसरे बच्चे एक घेरे में बैठकर कहानियाँ और अनुभव साझा कर रहे हैं। बच्चों का एक समूह कैंप काउंसलर की मदद से सादा खाना बनाना सीख रहा है। पास में, कुछ बच्चे शाम के टैलेंट शो के लिए अपने डांस मूव्स का अभ्यास कर रहे हैं। क्राफ्ट एरिया में, वे दोस्ती के कंगन बना रहे हैं। उनमें से कई प्रकृति की दुनिया की खोज कर रहे हैं। कुल मिलाकर, हर कोई अपने समय का आनंद ले रहा है।

playing, running, shouting, painting, sitting, sharing, learning, practicing, making, exploring, enjoying

SPEAK ENGLISH

Let us have the view of the social camp. The children are playing various games together. They are running around the playground, laughing and shouting with

joy. Some kids are painting colorful pictures under the shade of the trees.

Others are sitting in a circle, sharing stories and experiences. A group of children is learning to cook simple meals with the help of a camp counselor. Nearby, a few kids are practicing their dance moves for the evening talent show. In the craft area, they are making friendship bracelets. A bunch of them are exploring the world of nature. Overall, everyone is enjoying their time.

Give your presentation and tell what five other activities the children are doing at social camp.

GET SET GO

चलिए अब प्रैक्टिस के लिए तैयार हो जाइये

आप को आगे दिए गए सभी paragraph को एक एक करके पहले हिंदी में पढ़ना है और साथ में उस को मौखिक रूप से इंग्लिश में बोलने की कोशिश करनी है। क्योंकि सभी paragraph एक ही Present Continuous Tense / काल में लिखे गए है, 31 paragraphs प्रैक्टिस करते करते आप इस Tense को बेहतर ढंग से समझ पाओगे और आसानी से बोल पाओगे। प्रतिदिन एक अध्याय का अभ्यास करें और इस पुस्तक को एक महीने में पूरा करें।

सूरज धीरे-धीरे उग रहा है, क्षितिज पर एक गर्म सुनहरी चमक बिखेर रहा है। पक्षी खुशी से चहचहा रहे हैं, नए दिन का स्वागत कर रहे हैं। ओस की बूंदें घास पर चमक रही हैं, जो सुबह की कोमल रोशनी को प्रतिबिंबित कर रही हैं। फूल अपनी पंखुड़ियाँ खोल रहे हैं, जो जीवंत रंगों को प्रकट कर रही हैं। एक हल्की हवा पेड़ों की पत्तियों को सरसराहट कर रही है। पास में, एक झरना चुपचाप बह रहा है, इसका पानी सूरज की रोशनी में चमक रहा है।

rising, casting, chirping, greeting, glistening, reflecting, opening, revealing, rustling, flowing, sparkling.

The sun is rising slowly, casting a warm golden glow over the horizon. Birds are chirping cheerfully, greeting the new day. Dewdrops are glistening on the grass, reflecting the soft morning light. Flowers are opening their petals, revealing vibrant colors. A gentle breeze is rustling the leaves of the trees. Nearby, a stream is flowing quietly, its water is sparkling in the sunlight.

Make Sentences

Horizon, Dewdrops, Petals, Vibrant colors, A gentle breeze, Sunlight

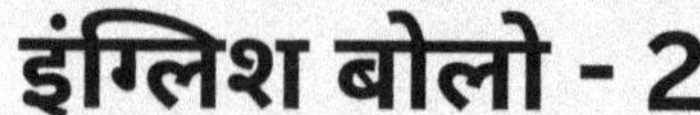

मैं अपनी दादी के साथ अक्सर मंदिर आता हूँ। आज, यह यात्रा मुझे उत्साह से भर रही है। पुजारी शांत स्वर में उपदेश दे रहे हैं। भक्तगण आँखें बंद करके बैठे हैं, और शांतिपूर्ण वातावरण में डूबे हुए हैं।

घंटियों की हल्की आवाज़ हवा में गूंज रही है, जो एक ऐसा संगीत बना रही है जो कानों को संगीत जैसा लगता है। मंत्रों के उच्चारण की ध्वनि पूरे हॉल में गूंज रही है। अगरबत्तियाँ जल रही हैं, और उनका मीठा-महक वाला धुआँ हल्की हवा की तरह चारों ओर फैल रहा है। मेरी दादी मुझे घंटियाँ बजाने, मंत्र पढ़ने और वेदी पर फूल चढ़ाने के लिए कह रही हैं। सच कहूँ तो, मैं बेसब्री से प्रसाद का इंतज़ार कर रहा हूँ, यही असली वजह है कि मैं अपने बड़ों के साथ उत्सुकता से मंदिर जाता हूँ।

Filling, preaching, sitting, creating, echoing, burning, drifting, asking, waiting

Speak English - 2

I come to the temple quite often with my granny. Today, the visit is filling me with exuberance. The priest is preaching with a calm voice. The devotees are sitting with their eyes closed, soaking in the peaceful atmosphere. The gentle ringing of bells is filling the air, creating a melody that feels like music to the ears. The sound of mantras being recited is echoing throughout the hall. Incense sticks are burning, their sweet-smelling smoke drifting around like a gentle breeze. My grandmother is asking me to ring the bells, recite the mantras, and place flowers at the altar. Honestly speaking, I am anxiously waiting for the prasadam, which is the real reason I eagerly accompany my elders to the temple.

Make Sentences
Exuberance, lullaby, devotees, melody, almighty

एक प्रसिद्ध कहावत है कि भूखे पेट सुन नहीं सकते। आज घर पर भी यही दृश्य है और सब कुछ अस्त-व्यस्त है ! हमारे माता-पिता  के चले जाने के कारण मेरी छोटी बहन भूख से तड़प रही है, जैसे वह पाषाण युग से ही भूखी रही हो।वह रो रही है, इतनी भूखी कि शीतनिद्रा में पड़े भालू की तरह रो रही है, और मेरी एक भी बात पर ध्यान नहीं दे रही है। मैं रसोई में जाकर कुछ स्वादिष्ट बनाने की कोशिश कर रहा हूँ, इस से पहले कि वह भूख हड़ताल पर बैठ जाए!

saying, chaos, starving, crying, hibernation, paying heed, rushing

There is a famous saying that a hungry stomach cannot hear. The same is a scene at home today and it is all chaos! With our folks away, my little sister is starving like she has been hungry since the Stone Age. She is crying her eyes out, as hungry as a bear in hibernation, and she is not paying heed to my any word. I am rushing to the kitchen to whip up something tasty before she stages a hunger strike!

> **Tell who is working in kitchen in your home at this time and what she is cooking and how?**

मैं इस समय चिड़ियाघर में घूम रहा हूँ, और यह जगह उत्साह से गुलजार है। जंगल के राजा की एक झलक पाने के लिए उत्सुक लोग शेर की मांद की ओर उमड़ रहे हैं। बच्चे मैगपाई की तरह चहचहा रहे हैं, विदेशी जानवरों को देखकर रोमांचित हैं। बंदर एक डाल से दूसरी डाल पर झूल रहे हैं। हाथी अपने तालाब में छप-छप करते हुए खूब मौज-मस्ती कर रहे हैं। पक्षीशाला में एक जैसे पक्षी एक साथ झुंड बनाकर चहचहाहट और सीटियों की आवाज से कोलाहल मचा रहे हैं। चिड़ियाघर के रखवाले मधुमक्खियों की तरह व्यस्त हैं, जानवरों को खाना खिला रहे हैं और उनकी देखभाल कर रहे हैं। परिवार पिकनिक मना रहे हैं, जीवंत माहौल का आनंद ले रहे हैं। मैं जहां भी देखता हूं, लोग मुस्कुरा रहे हैं, अपने कैमरों में यादें कैद कर रहे हैं।

Walking, buzzing, flocking, chattering, swinging, splashing, flocking, creating, feeding, having, enjoying, smiling, capturing

Speak English - 4

I am currently walking through the zoo, and the place is buzzing with excitement. Visitors are flocking to the lion's den, eager to catch a glimpse of the king of the jungle. Kids are chattering like magpies, thrilled by the sight of exotic animals. The monkey are swinging from branch to branch. The elephants are having a whale of a time, splashing around in their pond. In the aviary, birds of a feather are flocking together, creating a cacophony of chirps and whistles. Zookeepers are busy as bees, feeding and caring for the animals. Families are having picnics, enjoying the vibrant atmosphere. Everywhere I look, people are smiling, capturing memories with their cameras.

दिन तप रहा है और मैं क्लास में बैठा हूँ, आखिरी घंटी का इंतज़ार कर रहा हूँ। आसमान में काले बादल छाए हुए हैं और बच्चे अपने पैरों को घसीटते हुए घर की ओर जा रहे हैं। बूंदाबांदी हो रही है और छतरियाँ बारिश के बाद मशरूम की तरह खुल रही हैं। वापस आने वाले छात्र उत्साहित महसूस कर रहे हैं, पोखरों में कूद रहे हैं और पानी में छप-छप कर रहे हैं, उमस भरे दिन की चिलचिलाती गर्मी से राहत पा रहे हैं। यह ऐसा पल है जो उन्हें पीछे मुड़कर देखने और यह सोचने पर मजबूर कर देगा कि, "स्कूल के दिन सबसे अच्छे दिन थे।"

Sitting, waiting, dragging, drizzling, opening, returning, feeling, jumping, splashing, getting,

The day is burning hot and I am sitting in class, waiting for the last bell. The sky is overcast with dark clouds as kids are dragging their feet home. It is drizzling and umbrellas are pop opening like mushrooms after rain. The returning students are feeling excited, jumping in puddles and splashing water, getting cool relief from the scorching heat of the humid day. This is the kind of moment that will make them look back and think, "School days were the best days."

मेरा परिवार एक पार्टी के लिए तैयार हो रहा है। मेरी बहन सजावट कर रही है, जिससे जगह उत्सव के माहौल में बदल रही है। माँ रसोई में है, अपने प्रसिद्ध ऐपेटाइज़र बना रही है और स्वादिष्ट सुगंध से वातावरण को भर रही है। पिता साउंड सिस्टम लगा रहे हैं, यह सुनिश्चित कर रहे हैं कि संगीत सभी को नाचने पर मजबूर कर दे। मेरा भाई बाहर है, बैठने की व्यवस्था और रोशनी की व्यवस्था कर रहा है। मैं सुनिश्चित कर रहा हूँ कि सब कुछ समय पर हो जाए। उत्साह बढ़ रहा है, और हम आगे एक शानदार रात की उम्मीद कर रहे हैं।

Getting ready, hanging up, whipping up, filling, setting up, making sure, arranging, ensuring, building, anticipating

Speak English - 6

My family is getting ready for a party. My sister is hanging up decorations, turning the place into a festive wonderland. Mother is in the kitchen, whipping up her famous appetizers and filling the air with delicious aromas. Father is setting up the sound system, making sure the music will get everyone dancing. My brother is outside, arranging the seating and lighting. I am ensuring that everything get done on time. The excitement is building, and we are anticipating a fantastic night ahead.

जॉय जेसिका से पूछ रहा है कि क्या वह इस सप्ताहांत पिकनिक पर जा रही है। जेसिका कह रही है कि उसे पता है कि यह बहुत मज़ेदार होने वाला है लेकिन यह वास्तव में उसके बस की बात नहीं है।

जॉय उससे कह रही है कि वह इसे मिस न करे क्योंकि वह कड़ी मेहनत कर रही है, इसलिए उसे एक ब्रेक की ज़रूरत है। जेसिका शामिल नहीं हो रही है। जेसिका उसे शानदार पिकनिक की शुभकामनाएँ दे रही है और उम्मीद कर रही है कि इस सप्ताहांत मूसलाधार बारिश न हो। जॉय उँगलियों को क्रॉस करके बैठा है और प्यारे सप्ताहांत के लिए प्रार्थना कर रहा है।

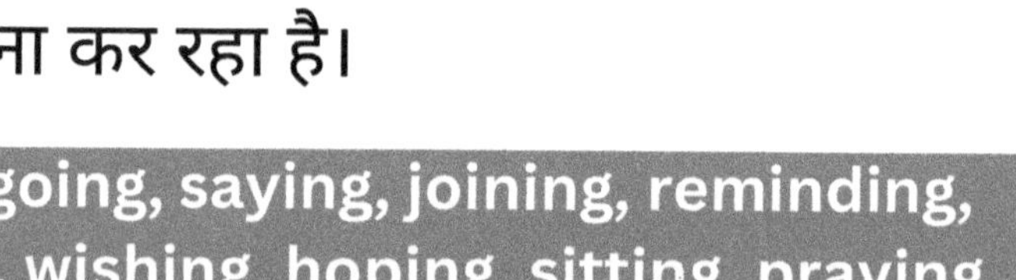

Asking, going, saying, joining, reminding, assuring, wishing, hoping, sitting, praying

Speak English - 7

Joy is asking Jessica if she is going to the picnic this weekend. Jessica is saying that she knows it is going to be a lot of fun but it is really not her cup of tea.

Joy is asking her not to miss it as she has been working like a dog, so she needs a break. Jessica is not joining. Jessica is wishing him fantastic picnic and hoping, it doesn't rain cats and dogs this weekend. Joy is sitting with fingers crossed and praying for the lovely weekend.

UNDERSTAND THE USE OF IDIOMS

Cup of tea, work like a dog, need a break, rain cat and dog, finger crossed

इंग्लिश बोलो - 8

सुबह के आठ बजे हैं और स्कूल में बहुत सारी गतिविधियाँ चल रही हैं। छात्र पैदल या बस से स्कूल

पहुँच रहे हैं। सभी छात्र अपनी वर्दी में बहुत स्मार्ट लग रहे हैं और वे अपने स्कूल की एकरूपता को दर्शा रहे हैं। छात्र अपनी पसंदीदा सीट पाने के

को दर्शा रहे हैं। छात्र अपनी पसंदीदा सीट पाने के लिए अपनी कक्षाओं में भाग रहे हैं और इस बीच, वे अपने शिक्षकों और अपने दोस्तों से मिल रहे हैं और उनका अभिवादन कर रहे हैं। वे आज कक्षाओं में अपने शिक्षकों से प्राप्त होने वाले नए ज्ञान के लिए बहुत उत्साहित दिख रहे हैं। स्कूल में सुबह का समय सुंदर होता है और वे छात्र भाग्यशाली होते हैं जिन्हें शिक्षा के मंदिर में प्रवेश करने का मौका मिलता है।

buzzing, reaching, looking, rushing, meeting, greeting, looking

Speak English - 8

It is eight in the morning and the school is buzzing with great activities. The students are reaching the school by walk or by bus. 

All the students are looking very smart in their uniform and they are reflecting the uniformity of their school. The students are rushing to their classes to get their favorite seats and in the mean while, they are also meeting and greeting their teachers and their friends. They are looking very excited for the new knowledge which they are going to acquire from their teachers in the classes today. The morning time in the school is beautiful and lucky are students who get a chance to step in the temple of learning.

> **What activities are going on in your class right now?**

खरगोश और कछुआ दौड़ रहे हैं और उत्साह साफ़ झलक रहा है। खरगोश बिजली की तरह तेज़ी से आगे बढ़ रहा है, जबकि कछुआ घोंघे की गति से आगे बढ़ रहा है। कछुए की धीमी शुरुआत के बावजूद, वह एक चट्टान की तरह स्थिर है और एक समान गति बनाए हुए

है। खरगोश पहले से ही सांस ले रहा है, यह मानते हुए कि जीत उसकी झोली में है। इस बीच, कछुआ एक पैर दूसरे के आगे रख रहा है, यह साबित करते हुए कि धीरे-धीरे और स्थिरता से दौड़ जीती जाती है। जैसे-जैसे कछुआ फिनिश लाइन के करीब पहुँच रहा है, यह स्पष्ट हो रहा है कि जल्दबाजी बेकार है और कमज़ोर व्यक्ति जीत सकता है।

Running, sprinting, lightning, plodding, maintaining, taking, assuming, putting, proving, reaching

Speak English - 9

The rabbit and the tortoise are running a race, and the excitement is palpable. The rabbit is sprinting ahead, as fast as lightning, while the tortoise is plodding along at a snail's pace. Despite the tortoise's slow start, it is steady as a rock, maintaining a consistent pace. The rabbit is already taking a breather, assuming victory is in the bag. Meanwhile, the tortoise is putting one foot in front of the other, proving that slow and steady wins the race. As the tortoise is reaching inches closer to the finish line, it becomes clear that haste makes waste and the underdog can triumph.

Make Sentences

as fast as lightning, at a snail's pace, steady as a rock, victory is in the bag, slow and steady wins the race, haste makes waste, the underdog can triumph.

मैं पहली बार रसोई में हूँ और फ्राइड राइस बनाने की कोशिश करने जा रहा हूँ। मैं सब्ज़ियों को सावधानी से काट रहा हूँ, इस डर से कि कहीं मैं खुद को न काट लूँ। जब मैं पैन में तेल गरम कर रहा हूँ, तो मेरे हाथ थोड़े काँप रहे हैं।

मैं लहसुन और अदरक डाल रहा हूँ, उम्मीद है कि मैं उन्हें जला न दूँ। अब, मैं सब्ज़ियों को समान रूप से पकाने के लिए उत्सुकता से हिला रहा हूँ। मैं चावल को पैन में डाल रहा हूँ, हर बार हिलाने पर मेरा दिल तेज़ी से धड़क रहा है। जैसे ही मैं सोया सॉस डाल रहा हूँ, मैं प्रार्थना कर रहा हूँ कि स्वाद अच्छी तरह से मिल जाए। अंत में, मैं फ्राइड राइस का स्वाद ले रहा हूँ ।

Making, chopping, fearing, heating, shaking, adding, stirring, pouring, pounding, praying, tasting,

Speak English - 10

I am in the kitchen for the first time and going to try my hand at making fried rice. I am chopping the vegetables carefully, fearing I may not cut myself. As I am heating the oil in the pan,

my hands are shaking a little. I am adding the garlic and ginger, hoping I don't burn them. Now, I am stirring in the vegetables anxiously to cook evenly. I am pouring the rice into the pan, my heart is pounding with each stir. As I am adding the soy sauce, I am praying the flavors blend well. Finally, I am tasting the fried rice.

Tell what you are going to try in kitchen today

Practice Role-Play

1. At the Airport:

Situation: Two friends are waiting at the airport, discussing what they and others around them are doing.

Example: "I am checking the flight status, and she is buying snacks."

2. Planning a Surprise Party:

Situation: Friends are organizing a surprise party for someone, discussing what each person is currently handling.

Example: "I am decorating the room, and he is baking the cake."

3. At the Café:

Situation: Two people are sitting in a café, observing other customers and talking about what everyone is doing.

Example: "I am drinking coffee, and she is reading a newspaper."

Practice Role-Play

1. **At the Zoo**

Scenario: Two children are visiting the zoo and talking about what the animals are doing. The conversation is about observing the animals in action.

Example Dialogue:

    a. "The lion is sleeping. What is the monkey doing?"

    b. "The monkey is swinging from the tree!"

2. Getting Ready for School

Scenario: Two siblings are getting ready for school in the morning. They are talking about the different things they are doing to prepare.

Example Dialogue:

    a. "I am brushing my teeth. What are you doing?"

    b. "I am packing my school bag."

3. Shopping with Parents

Scenario: A child is at the grocery store with a parent, talking about what they are buying. The conversation focuses on the actions of shopping.

Example Dialogue:

    a. "I am putting apples in the cart. What are you doing?"

    b. "I am choosing some bananas."

Mother: Joy, you're always playing games! Aren't you supposed to do your homework?

Joy: Mom, I know, but I'm just relaxing a bit. I'll do it later.

Mother: Later? You always say that! Right now, you're wasting precious time.

Joy: I'm not wasting it, Mom. I just need a break.

Mother: Look, I'm not against breaks, but your homework is waiting.

Joy : I am planning to do it before I go out to play with my friends.

Mother : What about the little chores lying pending in your room. Like, your study table is not well set, pillows are lying on floor, your pair of shoes and slippers are making your room look unmanaged.

Joy: Okay, okay. I'll start in a few minutes. Why worry so much?

Mother: Because you're forming a habit of delaying things, Joy. You aren't respecting time, and that worries me.

Joy: Alright, Mom. I'm starting all right now. See, I'm trying to be responsible.

Practice Conversation

Receptionist: Sir, I'm noticing that the phone lines are constantly breaking down, and it's affecting my work.

Manager: I understand. I'm seeing more complaints about missed calls. What else is happening?

Receptionist: Clients are often waiting because the seating area is getting too crowded, and I'm struggling to manage them.

Manager: I'm realizing how this might create a poor impression. Are you experiencing issues with any other equipment?

Receptionist: Yes, I'm dealing with a malfunctioning printer daily. It's slowing down my tasks and creating a backlog.

Manager: Alright, I'm making a note of these problems.

Receptionist: Sir, i need more organized workspace. Files are piling up, and I'm finding it difficult to locate documents quickly.

Manager: I'm understanding your concerns now, and I'm planning to address these infrastructure issues soon.

Practice Conversation

Sister: I am really worried about our garden. The roses are disappearing every day!

Brother: Yeah, I noticed that too. I think Tinko is the one messing with it.

Sister: He is always plucking the flowers and throwing trash around. It is so annoying!

Brother: I am keeping an eye on him now. He is sneaking around as if no one notices.

Sister: Look! He's bending down to grab another rose. He's not even being careful.

Brother: I'm recording him this time. He needs to see we're watching him.

Sister: Great idea! Let's show him the proof, and maybe he will finally stop. Let's catch him in the act.

Sister: Good idea! Then he can not deny it. Maybe he will stop once we show him the proof.

Mother: "It's quite cloudy today, dear. Don't forget to carry an umbrella!"

Daughter: "Oh, Mom, I'll be fine. I don't think it'll rain that much."

Mother: "Better safe than sorry. Just take it along. You'll thank me later."

Daughter: "Mom, really, it's just extra weight. I'll manage without it!"

Later, on her way back, it starts pouring...

Daughter: muttering to herself "Oh no! It's raining so hard! I should've listened to Mom!"

She sees other kids around her with umbrellas, happily skipping through the rain.

Daughter: "They all have umbrellas... Look at me, drenched from head to toe!"

Back home, she sneezes as she enters the house.

Mother: "Achoo! Look at you, completely soaked! Didn't I tell you to take an umbrella?"

Daughter: sheepishly "Yes, Mom, you were right. I should've listened to you."

Mother: "Maybe next time, you'll trust my advice, won't you?"

Daughter: "I definitely will! I've learned my lesson today!"

Make Your Notes

LET'S GO TO THE NEXT TENSE

PAST CONTINUOUS

पिछले निरंतर काल (Past Continuous Tense) का उपयोग उन कार्यों या घटनाओं को व्यक्त करने के लिए किया जाता है जो किसी निश्चित समय पर अतीत में हो रही थीं। इसमें कार्य के निरंतर होने का संकेत मिलता है।

इस काल की पहचान **"was/were"** सहायक क्रिया और **मुख्य क्रिया** के साथ **"ing"** जोड़कर होती है।

सकारात्मक वाक्य: सर्वनाम + was/were + क्रिया (ing जोड़कर) + बाकी वाक्य, उदाहरण:
बच्चे गेंद के पीछे दौड़ रहे थे। (The children were running after the ball.)

नकारात्मक वाक्य: सर्वनाम + was/were + not + क्रिया (ing जोड़कर) + बाकी वाक्य, उदाहरण: आप अपनी गलती स्वीकार नहीं कर रहे थे (You were not accepting your mistake.)

प्रश्नवाचक वाक्य: Was/Were + सर्वनाम + क्रिया (ing जोड़कर) + बाकी वाक्य? उदाहरण: क्या तुम मेरा इंतज़ार कर रहे थे? (Were you waiting for me?)

Practice Time 1

- वह अपनी किताबें ढूंढ रहा था। **(looking for)**
- बच्चे स्कूल जाने की तैयारी कर रहे थे। **(getting ready)**
- वे सड़क पर कचरा उठा रहे थे। **(picking up)**
- वह रात भर किसी समस्या पर काम कर रहा था। **(working on)**
- हम नए घर में रहने का प्रयास कर रहे थे। **(trying to, settle in)**
- वह अपनी नई परियोजना के लिए धन जुटा रहा था। **(raising funds)**
- बच्चे मैदान में खेल का आनंद ले रहे थे। **(playing around)**
- बच्चे अपना कमरा साफ कर रहे थे जब उनके दोस्त आए। **(cleaning up)**
- वह पूरे हफ्ते उस संगीत कार्यक्रम का इंतजार कर रही थी। **(looking forward to)**
- वह अपने छोटे भाई की देखभाल कर रहा था जब उसके माता-पिता बाहर थे। **(looking after)**
- मैं पिछले साल की छुट्टी के बारे में सोच रहा था। **(thinking about)**

English Version 1

- He **was looking for** his books.
- The children **were getting ready** for school.
- They **were picking up** trash on the street.
- He **was working on** a problem all night.
- We **were trying to settle in** the new house.
- She **was raising funds for** her new project.
- The kids **were playing around** in the field.
- The kids **were cleaning up** their room when their friends arrived.
- She **was looking forward to** the concert all week.
- He **was looking after** his younger brother while his parents were out.

Practice Time 2

- वह छुट्टियों के दौरान पौधों की देखभाल नहीं कर रहा था। **(looking after)**
- वे कल शाम जिम में कसरत नहीं कर रहे थे। **(working out)**
- वह पिछले साल कोई नया शौक नहीं अपना रही थी। **(picking up)**
- हम पिछले सप्ताहांत अपने दोस्तों के साथ नहीं घूम रहे थे। **(hanging out)**
- जब तुमने फोन किया तो मैं घर की सफाई नहीं कर रही थी। **(cleaning up)**
- वे उस समय किसी नए शहर में जाने के बारे में नहीं सोच रहे थे। **(thinking about)**
- जब उसकी माँ अंदर आई तो वह अपने कपड़े नहीं रख रही थी। **(putting away)**
- वह उस समय नई नौकरी के अवसरों पर विचार नहीं कर रहा था। **(looking into)**
- छुट्टियों के दौरान हम अपना काम पूरा नहीं कर पाए। **(catching up on)**
- पिछले महीने वह अपने स्वास्थ्य का ठीक से ख्याल नहीं रख रही थी। **(taking care)**

- He **was not looking after** the plants during the vacation.
- They **were not working out** at the gym yesterday evening.
- She **was not picking up** any new hobbies last year.
- We **weren't hanging out** with our friends last weekend.
- I **wasn't cleaning up** the house when you called.
- They **were not thinking about** moving to a new city at that time.
- She **was not putting away** her clothes when her mom walked in.
- He **was not looking into** the new job opportunities then.
- We **were not catching up on** our work during the holidays.
- She **was not taking care of** her health properly last month.

- क्या आप पिछले सप्ताहांत अपने पड़ोसी की बिल्ली की देखभाल कर रहे थे? **(looking after)**

- क्या वह बच्चों को स्कूल से लेने आया था जब बारिश शुरू हुई? **(picking up)**

- क्या वे पूरी रात एक साथ प्रोजेक्ट पर काम कर रहे थे? **(working on)**

- क्या वह उस समय अपनी नौकरी बदलने के बारे में सोच रही थी? **(thinking about)**

- क्या जब मैंने तुम्हें बुलाया तो तुम घर की सफाई कर रही थी? **(cleaning up)**

- क्या वह पिछले महीने की यात्रा का इंतजार कर रहा था? **(looking forward to)**

- क्या वे पिछवाड़े में पुराने शेड को तोड़ रहे थे? **(breaking down)**

- क्या वह पिछले सप्ताह फिर से अपना काम टाल रही थी? **(putting off)**

- क्या तुम पुराने फोटो एल्बम देख रही थी जब मैंने तुम्हें देखा? **(going through)**

- क्या वे मॉल में घूम रहे थे जब तुम उनसे मिली? **(hanging out)**

- **Were you looking after** your neighbor's cat last weekend?
- **Was he picking up** the kids from school when it started raining?
- **Were they working on** the project together all night?
- **Was she thinking about** changing her job at that time?
- **Were you cleaning up** the house when I called you?
- **Was he looking forward to** the trip last month?
- **Were they breaking down** the old shed in the backyard?
- **Was she putting off** her assignment again last week?
- **Were you going through** the old photo albums when I saw you?
- **Were they hanging out** at the mall when you met them?

पिछले रविवार को लिली बगीचे में खेल रही थी, फूलों को देख रही थी और तितलियों का पीछा कर रही थी। वह कांटेदार झाड़ियों के बहुत करीब चली गई थी। उसकी माँ उसे झाड़ियों के पास जाने से मना कर रही थी। लेकिन लिली अपनी माँ की सलाह को अनदेखा कर रही थी। अचानक, वह फिसल गई और झाड़ियों में गिर गई, उसके हाथों पर छोटी-छोटी खरोंचें आ गईं। इससे लिली ने सीखा कि "उन लोगों की बात सुनना बुद्धिमानी है जो हमारी परवाह करते हैं।"

Playing, exploring, chasing, wandering, forbidding, ignoring, tripped, fell, learned

Speak English - 11

Last Sunday, Lily was playing in the garden, exploring the flowers and chasing butterflies. She was wandering too close to the thorny bushes. Her mother was forbidding her to go close to the bushes. But Lily was ignoring her mother's advice. Suddenly, she tripped and fell into the bushes, got small scratches on her arms. From this, Lily learned that "It is wise to listen to those who care for us."

Make Sentences

Thorny bushes, Mother's advice, Small scratches

जॉय अपनी स्टडी टेबल पर बैठा हुआ पेंसिल से अपना होमवर्क कर रहा था, जबकि उसके पिता लिविंग रूम में थे, पेन से अपने ऑफिस के काम में व्यस्त थे। जॉय अपने पिता को देख रहा था, ईर्ष्या महसूस कर रहा था और चाहता था कि काश वह भी पेन से लिख पाता। वह चुपके से लिविंग रूम में घुस गया, अपने पिता की कलम ले ली और उससे अपना होमवर्क पूरा कर लिया। अगले दिन, होमवर्क चेक करते समय उसकी क्लास टीचर ने जॉय के पेन से किए गए काम को देखा। वह गुस्सा हो रही थी और उसे समझा रही थी कि शुरुआती कक्षाओं में आसानी से सुधार करने और गलतियों से सीखने के लिए पेंसिल का इस्तेमाल करना कितना ज़रूरी है। यह जॉय के लिए एक अच्छा सबक था। उसने खुद से वादा किया कि जब तक वह पेन के लिए तैयार नहीं हो जाता, तब तक वह पेंसिल का इस्तेमाल करता रहेगा। कहावत है, "धैर्य एक गुण है।"

Joy was sitting at his study table, doing his homework with a pencil while his father was in the living room, busy with his office work using a pen. Joy was watching his father, feeling envious and wishing he could write with a pen too. He was sneaking into the living room, taking his father's pen, and completing his homework with it. The next day, his class teacher while checking homework noticed Joy's work done in pen. She was getting angry and explaining to him the importance of using a pencil in the early classes for easy correction and learning from mistakes. It was a good lesson for Joy. He promised himself to stick to using a pencil until he was ready for a pen. The saying goes, "Patience is a virtue."

मैं स्कूल से घर लौट रहा था जब मैंने एक आवारा बिल्ली का बच्चा देखा जो सड़क के किनारे म्याऊँ कर रहा था। उसे बिल्ली के बच्चे पर तरस आया, मैंने उसे उठाया और जब मैं उसे घर ले जा रहा था, तो मैंने उसे कुछ खाना और पानी दिया, यह सुनिश्चित करते हुए कि वह आरामदायक है। अगले दिन, मैं बिल्ली के बच्चे के मालिक को खोजने में मदद करने के लिए पोस्टर लगा रहा था। दयालु होने से, टॉमी ने दिखाया कि "दयालुता मायने रखती है", क्योंकि आभारी मालिक ने अपने खोए हुए पालतू जानवर को पाया और उदारता से उसका धन्यवाद किया।

Walking, meowing, carrying, making, putting,

I was walking home from school when I saw a stray kitten who was meowing by the side of the road. He felt sorry for the kitten, I picked it up and when I was carrying it home, I fed him with some food and water, making sure it was comfortable. The next day, I was putting up posters to help find the kitten's owner.

By being kind, Tommy showed that "kindness matters," as the grateful owner found their lost pet and thanked him generously.

Treating others with kindness makes the world a better place and often brings kindness in return.

अपने कम्फर्ट जोन से बाहर निकलने पर अक्सर सबसे यादगार अनुभव होते हैं। मेरे साथ भी ऐसा ही हुआ है। मैं एक हवाई जहाज़ में बैठा था, मुझे डर लग रहा था क्योंकि

यह मेरी पहली हवाई यात्रा थी। दो बहनें खिड़की वाली सीट के लिए लड़ रही थीं, जिससे हंगामा हो रहा था। एक बूढ़ी महिला अपना हैंडबैग रखने से मना कर रही थी, उसे अपनी जान बचाने के लिए पकड़े हुए थी। एक बूढ़ा आदमी घुटन महसूस कर रहा था, अख़बार से हवा कर रहा था। पायलट स्वागत घोषणा कर रहा था जबकि एयरहोस्टेस मुस्कुराते हुए ड्रिंक सर्व कर रही थी और घबराए हुए यात्रियों को शांत कर रही थी। लोग हंस रहे थे और बातें कर रहे थे, जिससे मेरी घबराहट कम हो रही थी। धीरे-धीरे, मुझे लगने लगा था कि मैं उड़ान को आसानी से ले सकता हूँ।

Stepping out, sitting, fighting, refusing, clutching, feeling, fanning, making, serving, calming, laughing, chatting, helping, beginning

Stepping out of our comfort zone often leads to the most memorable experiences. I too have had one. I was sitting in an airplane, feeling scared since it was my first air journey. Two sisters were fighting for the window seat, causing a ruckus. An old lady was refusing to place away her handbag, clutching it for dear life. An old man was feeling suffocated, fanning himself with a newspaper. The pilot was making a welcome announcement while the airhostess was serving drinks with a smile and calming nervous flyers. People were laughing and chatting, which was helping to ease my nerves. Slowly, I was beginning to feel like I could take the flight in stride.

इंग्लिश बोलो - 15

कल, मैं और मेरा दोस्त चिड़ियाघर में घूम रहे थे। बंदर पेड़ों पर कूद रहे थे और एक दूसरे पर चिल्ला रहे थे। शेर अपने बाड़े में दहाड़ रहे थे, जबकि हाथी अपनी सूंड से पानी फेंक रहे थे। मोर अपने पंख फैला रहे थे और मधुर स्वर में गा

रहे थे। माहौल वाकई अद्भुत था। शेर जोर से दहाड़ रहे थे और हाथी अपने बड़े-बड़े कान फड़फड़ा रहे थे और चिंघाड़ रहे थे। बत्तखें कूं-कूं कर रही थीं और भेड़ें मिमिया रही थीं। पक्षी चहचहा रहे थे और पूरा चिड़ियाघर उनके गीतों से गूंज रहा था। घोड़े हिनहिना रहे थे और बंदर उछल-कूद करते हुए शोर मचा रहे थे। ये सभी जानवर अपने-अपने अनोखे तरीके से आवाजें निकाल रहे थे और ऐसा लग रहा था जैसे ये सभी किसी भव्य संगीत समारोह का हिस्सा हों।

Speak English - 15

Yesterday, my friend and I were walking around the zoo. The monkeys were jumping on the trees and shouting at each other. The lions were roaring in their enclosure, while the elephants were splashing water with their trunks. The peacocks were spreading their feathers and singing in a beautiful voice. The atmosphere was truly amazing. The lions were roaring loudly and the elephants were flapping their big ears and trumpeting. Ducks were quacking and sheep were bleating. Birds were chirping, and the whole zoo was echoing with their songs. Horses were neighing, and monkeys were making noise while jumping around. All these animals were making sounds in their own unique ways, and it felt like they were all part of a grand concert.

How many different animal sounds are you familiar with?

इंग्लिश बोलो - 16

"समय और ज्वार किसी का इंतजार नहीं करते।" क्षणभंगुर समय का महत्व समझना बहुत ज़रूरी है। पिछले महीने मेरी परीक्षाएँ थीं और मुझसे समय प्रबंधन करने के लिए कहा गया था। जब मैं अपना समय प्रबंधित कर रहा था,

तो मैं अपनी प्राथमिकताओं को व्यवस्थित करने की कोशिश कर रहा था। मैं हर दिन एक सूची बना रहा था और उसे पूरा करने की कोशिश कर रहा था। जब मैं पढ़ रहा था, तो 

मैं ध्यान केंद्रित करने के लिए अपना फ़ोन दूर रख रहा था। मैं अपने असाइनमेंट समय पर जमा कर रहा था और अपनी दिनचर्या में नियमित ब्रेक ले रहा था। मैं अपने दोस्तों और परिवार के साथ बिताने के लिए भी समय निकाल रहा था। इस तरह, मैं अपनी पढ़ाई और निजी जीवन को संतुलित कर रहा था।

Was asked, trying, making, studying, keeping, submitting, taking, making, balancing

Speak English - 16

"Time and tide wait for none." It is highly important to value the fleeting time. Last month I had my exams and I was asked to have time management.

When I was managing my time, I was trying to organize my priorities. I was making a list every day and trying to complete it. When I was studying, I was keeping my phone away to stay focused.

I was submitting my assignments on time and taking regular breaks in my routine. I was also making time to spend with my friends and family. In this way, I was balancing my studies and personal life.

माँ मछली नदी में तैर रही थी, अपनी बेटी को खाना ढूँढ़ना सिखा रही थी। वह उसे पानी के बाहर की बड़ी दुनिया के बारे में और ऊपर से गिरने वाले खाने के बारे में भी चेतावनी दे रही थी, जो मछली पकड़ने वाले का चारा हो सकता है। "चारे में एक हुक होगा," वह कह रही थी, "और अगर यह तुम्हारे मुँह में फँस गया, तो तुम फँस जाओगे। वह आदमी तुम्हें चाकू से काटेगा, जलते हुए तेल में डालेगा, तुम्हें भूनेगा और खा जाएगा।" छोटी मछली सुन रही थी लेकिन वह भोजन का स्वाद लेने के मौके का इंतज़ार कर रही थी। जब माँ मछली आस-पास नहीं थी, तो उसने पानी में गिरते हुए खाने को ले लिया। जल्द ही, वह फँस गई। अब उसने चाकू, उबलता हुआ तेल और आदमी को देखा लेकिन अब उसके ज्ञान का कोई मूल्य नहीं था।

Swimming, teaching, warning, dropping, saying, listening, waiting,

The mother fish was swimming in the river, teaching her daughter how to find food. She was warning her about the big world outside the water and also about the food dropping in from above, which could be bait from a fish catcher. "The bait will have a hook," she was saying, "and if it gets stuck in your mouth, you'll be hooked up. The man will cut you open with a knife, put you in burning oil, fry you, and eat you." The baby fish was listening but she was waiting for the chance to taste the food. When the mother fish was not around, she took the food dropping in the water. Soon, she was hooked up. Now she saw the knife, the boiling oil and the man but her knowledge had no value now.

Knowledge is Power !

जॉय: "जैसिका, क्या तुम कल परीक्षा के लिए पढ़ाई कर रही थी?"

जैसिका: "हाँ, मैं पूरी दोपहर पढ़ाई कर रही थी। क्या तुम बास्केटबॉल का अभ्यास कर रहे थे?"

जॉय: "मैं कर रहा था, लेकिन मैं अपने भाई की होमवर्क में भी मदद कर रहा था।"

जैसिका: "मैं इसके बारे में सुन रही थी। उसे गणित में दिक्कत आ रही थी, है न?"

जॉय: "हाँ वह संघर्ष कर रहा था, लेकिन शाम तक वह शांत और आत्मविश्वासी महसूस कर रहा था।"

Studying, practicing, helping, hearing, struggling, feeling

Speak English - 18

Joy: "Jassica, were you studying for the exam yesterday?"

Jassica: "Yes, I was studying all afternoon. Were you practicing basketball?"

Joy: "I was, but I was also helping my brother with his homework."

Jassica: "I was hearing about that. He was struggling with math, right?"

Joy: "Yes, he was, but he was feeling relaxed and confident by the evening."

Write a conversation between Joy and Jassica.

इंग्लिश बोलो - 19

जॉय: "जैसिका, क्या तुम कल कुकीज़ बेक करने की कोशिश कर रही थी?"

जैसिका: "हाँ, मैं कर रही थी, लेकिन कुकीज़ कोयले में तब्दील हो रही थीं!"

जॉय: "मैं घर में जली हुई चीनी की खुशबू फैलती देख रही थी।"

जैसिका: "मैं उन्हें बचाने की पूरी कोशिश कर रही थी, लेकिन वे बचाने लायक नहीं थीं।"

जॉय: "मैं हँस रहा था, कल्पना कर रहा था कि तुम ओवन से जूझ रही हो।"

जैसिका: "ओवन मेरे खिलाफ़ साजिश कर रहा था, मैं कसम खाती हूँ!"

जॉय: "इस बीच, मैं एक बढ़िया पिज़्ज़ा खा रहा था। ज़्यादा सुरक्षित विकल्प!"

attempting, metamorphosing, envisaging, chuckling, battling, conspiring, devouring

Joy: "Jassica, were you attempting to bake cookies yesterday?"

Jassica: "Yes, I was, but the cookies were metamorphosing into charcoal!"

Joy: "I was envisaging the aroma of burnt sugar wafting through the house."

Jassica: "I was desperately trying to salvage them, but they were unsalvageable."

Joy: "I was chuckling, imagining you battling with the oven."

Jassica: "The oven was conspiring against me, I swear!"

Joy: "Meanwhile, I was devouring a perfectly good pizza. Much safer choice!"

परदे के पीछे, यह एक पागलखाना था। जॉय और उसके दोस्त बच्चों के फैंसी ड्रेस शो के लिए तैयार हो रहे थे। बच्चे मधुमक्खियों की तरह भिनभिना रहे थे, बेतहाशा वेशभूषा ठीक कर रहे थे। कुछ लोग रॉकिंग कुर्सियों से भरे कमरे में एक लंबी पूंछ वाली बिल्ली की तरह घबराए हुए थे। शिक्षक अंतिम समय की बारीकियों को ठीक करते हुए, इधर-उधर भाग रहे थे। जॉय अपनी टोपी को रखने की कोशिश कर रहा था, लिली अपने परी के पंख ठीक कर रही थी, और टॉम, जो बंदर की तरह कपड़े पहने हुए था, अपने पेट को खुजला रहा था। पर्दा उठने ही वाला था कि बच्चे मंच को ठीक से सजा रहे थे। हर कोई नट फैक्ट्री में गिलहरी की तरह बेचैन था, शो शुरू होने के लिए उत्साहित था।

Behind the curtain, it was a madhouse. Joy and his friends were getting ready for the children's fancy dress show. Kids were buzzing around like bees, frantically adjusting costumes. Some were as nervous as a long-tailed cat in a room full of rocking chairs. Teachers were running around fixing last-minute details. Joy was trying to keep his hat on, Lilly was fixing her fairy wings, and Tom, dressed as a monkey, was scratching his tummy. Kids were setting the stage right as the curtain was about to roll up. Everyone was as jittery as a squirrel in a nut factory, excited for the show to start.

- **Madhouse:** A place full of chaos and noise,
- **Buzzing around like bees:** Moving around quickly and busily,
- **As nervous as a long-tailed cat in a room full of rocking chair**s: Extremely nervous or anxious,
- **As jittery as a squirrel in a nut factory:** Very nervous or excited, implying restlessness and high energy.

Granny: Joy, what were you doing in the garden?

Joy: I was trying to catch butterflies, Granny!

Granny: Oh, dear, you shouldn't have done that.

Joy: But they were so pretty! I wanted to keep one.

Granny: Butterflies were happiest when they were free. If you catch them, they may get hurt.

Joy: Really? I didn't think of that.

Granny: Yes, my boy. They need to fly and play in the flowers.

Joy: I guess you were right, Granny. I let them be.

Granny: That is a good decision, Joy. You could watch them without touching.

Joy: Okay, Granny, I would just enjoy their beauty from now on.

Joy: Dad, do you remember last Saturday?

Father: Yes, I do. What about it?

Joy: I was reading a book when you called me for dinner.

Father: Oh, right! And I was cooking your favorite dish at that time.

Joy: I noticed. While you were cooking, Mom was setting the table.

Father: Yes, and your sister was helping her. What were you doing after dinner?

Joy: I was finishing my homework, but I kept thinking about that dessert.

Father: I was cleaning up the kitchen when you came to ask for more.

Joy: Yeah, I couldn't resist. The cake was amazing!

Father: Son, I was noticing you were spending a lot of time on your phone. Were you reading anything interesting?

Son: No, Dad, I was just scrolling through videos. Everyone is watching them these days.

Father: I understand, but I was hoping you were reading books. Books were my best teachers when I was your age.

Son: Really? I thought books were boring.

Father: Not at all! I used to find new ideas, stories, and knowledge in books. You should try it.

Son: But books cost a lot, Dad.

Father: True, but remember, "A good book is a good friend." Do not be afraid to spend on them. They're worth every penny.

Son: Alright, Dad, maybe I'll start with one. I was just worried it might be a waste.

Father: You'll see it isn't. Books always taught me something new. They'll do the same for you.

Parent: I was noticing that Harry hasn't been well lately. He was studying for hours every day.

Teacher: Yes, I was seeing that too. He was really focused in class, but he needs time to relax as well.

Parent: I thought more studying would help him succeed. I was pushing him hard to excel.

Teacher: While it's important to study, remember, "All work and no play makes Jack a dull boy." He needs time for other activities too.

Parent: I understand, but I was worried he wouldn't do well without the extra effort.

Teacher: Harry was already doing great in his studies. Allowing him some free time will help him grow in other skills too.

Parent: I see your point. I will try to give him some space to enjoy his time and explore other interests.

Make Your Notes

Make Your Notes

LET'S

GO
TO
THE
NEXT TENSE

FUTURE CONTINUOUS

UNDERSTAND FUTURE CONTINUOUS

भविष्य में किसी निश्चित समय पर जारी रहने वाली क्रिया को व्यक्त करने के लिए भविष्य काल की निरंतरकालीन रचना का उपयोग किया जाता है। यह यह बताने के लिए प्रयोग होता है कि कोई व्यक्ति या वस्तु भविष्य में किसी निश्चित समय पर क्या कर रहा होगा।

जिस प्रकार वर्तमान हमें बताता है कि कोई कार्य हो रहा है भूतकाल से हमें पता चलता है कि कोई कार्य हो रहा था | ठीक उसी प्रकार भविष्य कल से हमें पता चलता है कि भविष्य में कोई कार्य हो रहा होगा | इस बात को समझने के लिए हम सभी तीन Tenses के examples ले सकते हैं जैसे कि बच्चे क्रिकेट खेल रहे हैं, बच्चे मैच खेल रहे थे और भविष्य में इसे हम कहेंगे कि बच्चे क्रिकेट खेल रहे होंगे | भविष्य में जो कार्य हो रहा होगा उसे Future Continuous Tense कहा जाता है

वाक्य संरचना:

- ○ Subject (कर्ता) + Helping verb (सहायक क्रिया) + Main verb root (मुख्य क्रिया का मूल रूप) + रहा/रही/रहे + होगा/होगी/होंगे
- ○ Example: वह पढ़ रहा होगा।

In English, "will" and "shall" are both used to indicate future actions or events, but they have slightly different usages and connotations. Here are the key points on when to use "will" and "shall":

Will

- **General Future Actions:** "Will" is used for general future actions or events.
  - Example: I will go to the store tomorrow.
- **Promises and Offers:** "Will" is often used to make promises or offers.
  - Example: I will help you with your homework.
- **Decisions Made at the Moment of Speaking:** "Will" is used when a decision is made at the moment of speaking.
  - Example: I think I will have the chicken for dinner.
- **Predictions:** "Will" is used to make predictions about the future.
  - Example: It will rain tomorrow.

Shall

- **Formal and Legal Contexts:** "Shall" is more formal and is often used in legal documents or formal writing.
  - Example: The tenant shall pay the rent by the first of each month.
- First Person Singular and Plural (I/We): **Traditionally, "shall" was used with "I" and "we" for future actions,** but this usage is becoming less common in modern English.
  - Example: We shall overcome this challenge.
- **Suggestions and Offers** (First Person): "Shall" can be used to make suggestions or offers when used with "I" or "we".
  - Example: Shall we go for a walk?
- **Obligations or Strong Determination:** In formal contexts, "shall" can express obligations or strong determination.
  - Example: You shall complete this task by tomorrow.

UNDERSTAND FUTURE CONTINUOUS

Positive Sentences
Example :

- शिक्षक कक्षा में पढ़ा रहे होंगे।
- छात्र अपने बोलने के कौशल में सुधार कर रहे होंगे।
- मेरा भाई अपने जीवन में अच्छे अवसर की तलाश कर रहा होगा।
- The teacher will be teaching in the class.
- The students will be improving their speaking skills.
- My brother will be looking for a good opportunity in his life.

Negative Sentences
Example :

- जॉय झूठ नहीं बोलेगा।
- लड़कियाँ अपना काम पूरा नहीं करेंगी।
- आपके शहर में भारी बारिश नहीं होगी।
- Joy will not be telling a lie.
- The girls will not be completing their assignment.
- It will not be raining heavily in your city.

UNDERSTAND FUTURE CONTINUOUS

Interrogative Sentences

Example:

- क्या बच्चे अपनी छुट्टियों का इंतज़ार कर रहे होंगे?
- क्या हमारी टीम जीत की ओर बढ़ रही होगी?
- क्या आपका परिवार इस सप्ताहांत कोई फिल्म देखने की योजना बना रहा होगा?
- Will children be waiting for their holidays ?
- Will our team be heading towards the victory ?
- Will your family be planning to watch a movie this weekend?

The future continuous tense is formed using "will be" + present participle (verb + -ing). For example, "I will be working."

- Our school will be celebrating its annual day next month.
- The weather will not be improving tomorrow according to the forecast.
- The scientist will be conducting an important experiment in the lab.
- Will the astrologer be predicting any major events for next year?
- The health department will not be issuing any new guidelines next week.
- The police will be patrolling the streets during the night.
- Will the trees be shedding their leaves in autumn?
- The sun will be setting later as summer approaches.
- My heart will be longing for you every day.
- Will the sun be shining brightly tomorrow morning?

- मैं अगले सप्ताह अपने पड़ोसी के कुत्ते की देखभाल कर रहा होगा। **(looking after)**
- वह अपने दोस्त को हवाई अड्डे से लेने आ रही होगी। **(picking up)**
- वे अगले महीने तक मीटिंग टाल रहे होंगे। **(putting off)**
- वह आज शाम जिम में कसरत कर रहा होगा। **(working out)**
- हम अगले सप्ताह नया कार्यालय स्थापित कर रहे होंगे। **(setting up)**
- आप दोपहर 3 बजे तक होटल में चेक-इन कर रहे होंगे। **(checking in)**
- बच्चे शनिवार को अपने कमरे साफ रहे होंगे। **(cleaning up)**
- मैं कल अपनी टीम के साथ रिपोर्ट पर चर्चा कर रहा होगा। **(going over)**
- अपनी बैठक के दौरान वह अपने सभी पुराने दोस्तों से मिलें रही होगी। **(catching up)**
- वे अगले मंगलवार को प्रयोगशाला में प्रयोग कर रहे होंगे। **(carrying out)**

- I **will be looking after** my neighbor's dog next week.
- She **will be picking up** her friend from the airport tomorrow.
- They **will be putting off** the meeting until next month.
- He **will be working out** at the gym this evening.
- We **will be setting up** the new office next week.
- You **will be checking in** at the hotel by 3 PM.
- The kids **will be cleaning up** their rooms on Saturday.
- I **will be going over** the report with my team tomorrow.
- She **will be catching up** with her old friends during her meeting.
- They **will be carrying out** the experiment in the lab next Tuesday.

Practice Time 2

- कामगार अपना काम पूरा करने से पहले आराम नहीं कर रहे होंगे। **(will not be taking rest)**
- बारिश होने के कारण पक्षी उड़ नहीं रहे होंगे। **(will not be flying)**
- शिक्षक द्वारा पढ़ाए जाने के कारण बच्चे कक्षा में शोर नहीं मचा रहे होंगे। **(will not be making a noise)**
- नेता जनता को बहका नहीं रहे होंगे। **(will not be beguiling)**
- राजा जनता के प्रति अपनी जिम्मेदारी की अनदेखी नहीं कर रहे होंगे। **(will not be ignoring)**
- माता-पिता बच्चों को उनके मौज-मस्ती के समय पढ़ाई करने के लिए मजबूर नहीं कर रहे होंगे। **(will not be forcing)**
- बारिश के कारण बच्चे पार्क में नहीं खेल पा रहे होंगे। **(will not be playing)**
- सर्दियाँ आने से पहले गौरैया अपना घोंसला नहीं बना रही होगी| **(will not be making)**

- The workers **will not be taking rest** before they complete their work.
- The birds **will not be flying** because it is raining.
- Children **will not be making a noise** in the class as the teacher is teaching them.
- The leaders **will not be beguiling** the masses.
- The king **will not be ignoring** his responsibility towards the masses.
- The parents **will not be forcing** the children to study during their fun time.
- The rain **will not be allowing** the children to play in the park.
- The sparrows **will not be making** their nest before the winter sets in.

- क्या आप सम्मेलन में भाग ले रहे होंगे? **(attending)**
- क्या वे इस गर्मी में यूरोप की यात्रा कर रहे होंगे? **(travelling)**
- क्या वह आज रात देर तक काम कर रही होगी? **(working)**
- क्या हम कल सुबह बैठक कर रहे होंगे? **(having a meeting)**
- क्या वह रविवार को मैच में खेल रहा होगा? **(playing)**
- क्या आप इस सप्ताहांत अपने दादा-दादी से मिलने जा रहे होंगे? **(visiting)**
- क्या वे अगले महीने नया उत्पाद लॉन्च कर रहे होंगे? **(launching)**
- क्या वह पूरी रात अपनी परीक्षाओं की तैयारी कर रही होगी? **(studying)**
- क्या हम साथ में आपका जन्मदिन मना रहे होंगे? **(celebrating)**
- क्या वह बाद में हमारे साथ रात के खाने में शामिल हो रहे होंगे? **(joining)**

- **Will you be attending** the conference?
- **Will they be traveling** to Europe this summer?
- **Will she be working** late tonight?
- **Will we be having** a meeting tomorrow morning?
- **Will he be playing** in the match on Sunday?
- **Will you be visiting** your grandparents this weekend?
- **Will they be launching** the new product next month?
- **Will she be studying** for her exams all night?
- **Will we be celebrating** your birthday together?
- **Will he be joining** us for dinner later?

चालाक लोमड़ी बहुत भूखी होगी। वह अपनी भूख मिटाने के लिए कुछ तलाश रही होगी। तभी वह एक पेड़ की डाली पर बैठे एक कौवे को देखेगी। कौवा आनंद के साथ बड़े टुकड़े में चीज़ खा रहा होगा। लोमड़ी का दिमाग घोड़े की तरह तेज़ दौड़ रहा होगा, और वह चीज़ का टुकड़ा पाने की योजना बना रही होगी। वह कौवे की प्रशंसा करते हुए कहेगी कि वह सबसे सुंदर पक्षी है और उसकी आवाज़ तो और भी मीठी होनी चाहिए। वह कौवे को गाने के लिए चोंच खोलने के लिए मना रही होगी। उसकी चालाक मंशा केवल स्वादिष्ट चीज़ का टुकड़ा हासिल करने की होगी।

Will be looking for, will spot, will be devouring, will be running, will be scheming, will be flattering, will be coaxing,

The clever fox will be very hungry. He will be looking for something to satisfy his hunger. He will spot a crow sitting on the branch of a tree. The crow will be devouring a large piece of cheese with sheer delight. The fox's mind will be running faster than a race horse and he will be scheming to get the piece of cheese. He will be flattering the crow by telling him that he is the most beautiful bird and his voice must be sweeter. He will be coaxing the crow to open his beak to sing. His sneaky intention will only be to grab the delicious piece of cheese.

जॉय, जो आज बीमार है, डिनर से पहले आइसक्रीम खाने की ज़िद कर रहा होगा, भले ही उसकी माँ उसे बार-बार मना कर रही होगी। वह इसे खाने पर अड़ा रहेगा, यह कहते 

हुए कि यह उसकी पसंदीदा है। इस बीच, उसकी माँ उसे डिनर के बाद तक इंतज़ार करने की सलाह दे रही होगी। वह समझा रही होगी कि पहले आइसक्रीम खाने से उसकी भूख खराब हो जाएगी और यह सेहत के लिए अच्छा नहीं है। लेकिन जॉय ज़िद करता रहेगा।

Will be insisting, will be adamant, will be advising, will be explaining, will keep persisting

Joy who is under bad weather today will be insisting on eating ice cream before dinner, despite his mother's repeated warnings. He will be adamant about having  it, claiming it is his favorite. Meanwhile, his mother will be advising him to wait until after dinner. She will be explaining that eating ice cream first will spoil his appetite and is not healthy. But Joy will keep persisting.

What three things children be insisting on during their summer vacation?

कल मेरे दोस्त के घर पार्टी होगी, लेकिन दुर्भाग्यवश मैं कुछ व्यक्तिगत कारणों से शामिल नहीं हो पाऊंगा। मुझे पता है कि सभी लोग पार्टी ड्रेस में पहुंच रहे

होंगे और मेज़बान उन्हें उत्साह के साथ स्वागत कर रही होगी। मेज़बान स्नैक्स सर्व कर रही होगी और मेहमान लिविंग रूम में कपल डांस का आनंद ले रहे होंगे। डिनर के दौरान, वे आरामदायक संगीत सुन रहे होंगे और खाने का स्वाद ले रहे होंगे। जैसे-जैसे रात बीत रही होगी, वे एक-दूसरे को शुभकामनाएं दे रहे होंगे और अपने घरों की ओर जा रहे होंगे।

Will not be attending, will be arriving, will be greeting, will be serving, will be enjoying, will be listening, will be exchanging

Tomorrow, there will be a party at my friend's house, but unfortunately, I won't be attending due to some personal reasons. I know everyone will be arriving in their party dresses and the host will be greeting them with excitement. The host will be serving snacks and the invitees will be enjoying the couple's dance in the living room. During dinner, they will be listening to relaxing music and relishing the food. As the night winds down, they will be exchanging good wishes and leaving for their homes.

How children will be celebrating Children's Day on 14th November?

भारत अपना 78वाँ स्वतंत्रता दिवस मना रहा होगा। पूरे देश में खुशी और उल्लास का माहौल होगा। विभिन्न स्तरों पर कुछ विशेष सांस्कृतिक कार्यक्रम हो रहे होंगे। जॉय स्कूल की परेड में भाग ले

रहा होगा। सभी छात्र समारोह में झंडे लहरा रहे होंगे और देशभक्ति के गीत गा रहे होंगे। प्रधानाचार्य देश के इतिहास और उपलब्धियों को सम्मानित करने के लिए एक भाषण दे रहे होंगे। वे अपने स्वतंत्रता सेनानियों के बलिदानों को याद कर रहे होंगे और एक स्वतंत्र देश के नागरिक होने पर गर्व महसूस कर रहे होंगे।

Will be going on, will be participating, will be waving, will be delivering, will be recalling, feeling proud

Speak English - 24

India will be celebrating its 78th Independence Day. There will be a vibe of joy and jubilation all around the country. Some special cultural programs will be going on at different levels. Joy will be participating in school march past. All the students will be waving flags and singing patriotic songs in the function. The principal will be delivering a speech to honor the nation's history and achievements. They will be recalling the sacrifices of their freedom fighters and feeling proud to be the citizens of a free nation.

> A hero is someone who understands the responsibility that comes with his freedom.
> – Bob Dylan

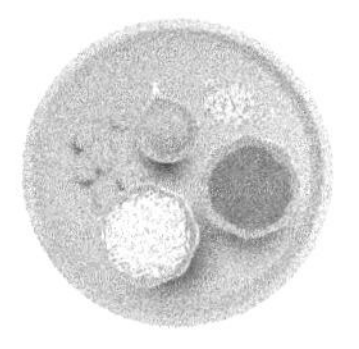

आज एक पर्व का दिन है। शिक्षक विद्यार्थियों को रक्षा बंधन के त्योहार के बारे में बता रहे होंगे। यह भाई-बहन के प्रेम के बंधन का उत्सव है। लोग इस विशेष दिन पर एक-दूसरे को शुभकामनाएं दे रहे होंगे। लड़कियाँ पूजा की थाली को फूलों, मिठाइयों, चावल, रंगोली, तिलक, अगरबत्ती और राखी से सजा रही होंगी। भाई-बहन बहुत खुश होंगे और दिन को यादगार बनाने के लिए हर संभव प्रयास कर रहे होंगे। जॉय की बहन भी अपने भाई की कलाई पर प्रेम के धागे बाँध रही होगी और उसे लंबे और स्वस्थ जीवन की शुभकामनाएँ दे रही होगी। जॉय अपनी बहन का हमेशा ध्यान रखने का वादा कर रहा होगा। वे एक-दूसरे को प्यारे उपहार दे रहे होंगे और अपने प्यार का इज़हार खुले दिल से कर रहे होंगे।

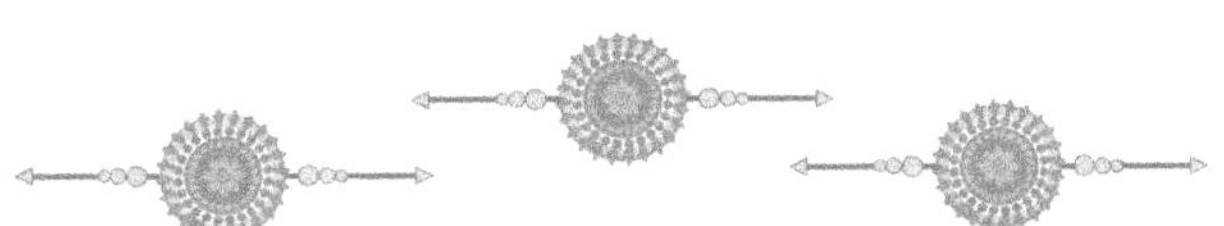

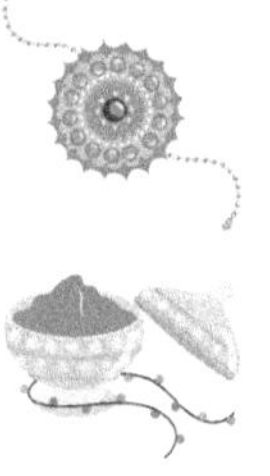

Speak English - 25

It is a festive day today. The teachers will be telling the students about the festival of Raksha Bandhan. It is a celebration of the bond of love between brothers and sisters. People will be exchanging warm wishes on this special day. The girls will be decorating the puja thali with flowers, sweets, rice, rangoli, tika, incense, and rakhi. Brothers and sisters will be feeling over the moon and doing everything to make the day unforgettable. Joy's sister, too, will be tying the threads of love on her brother's wrist, wishing him a long and healthy life. Joy will be pledging to always look out for his sister. They will be exchanging thoughtful gifts and wearing their hearts on their sleeves to express their love for each other.

जॉय बड़े होते हुए सेहतमंद खाने के महत्व के बारे में सीख रहा होगा। उनके शिक्षक उन्हें समझा रहे होंगे कि जंक फूड से बचना उनके स्वास्थ्य के लिए क्यों जरूरी है। जॉय यह जान रहा होगा कि जंक फूड मोटापा और कम ऊर्जा जैसी समस्याएं पैदा कर सकता है। चिप्स और मिठाइयों की बजाय, वह फल और सब्जियाँ चुन रहा होगा जो उसे ताकतवर और सक्रिय रखेंगे। उनके माता-पिता हर दिन उसे बेहतर खाने की आदतें अपनाने के लिए प्रोत्साहित कर रहे होंगे। जॉय जंक फूड से बचकर उन अच्छी आदतों का निर्माण कर रहा होगा जो जीवनभर उसके लिए लाभकारी होंगी। वह आज अपने शरीर की देखभाल करने के लिए भविष्य में खुद को धन्यवाद दे रहा होगा।

will be learning, will be explaining, will be discovering, will be choosing, will be encouraging, will be building, will be thanking

Joy will be learning about the importance of healthy eating as he grows up. His teachers will be explaining why avoiding junk food is crucial for his health. Joy will be discovering that junk food can cause problems like obesity and low energy levels. Instead of eating chips and candies, he will be choosing fruits and vegetables that will keep him strong and active. His parents will be encouraging him to make better food choices every day. By avoiding junk food, Joy will be building good habits that will benefit him throughout his life. He will be thanking himself later for taking care of his body today.

"Good food choices are good investments in your health."

मिंकू बंदर, जो कि आलसी है, जंगल में एक पेड़ से दूसरे पेड़ पर झूल रहा होगा, मज़े की तलाश में। वह व्यस्त गिलहरियों के पास चुपके से जाकर

उनके नट्स चुरा रहा होगा। मिंकू मेहनती चींटियों को तंग कर रहा होगा और उनका खाना इधर-उधर बिखेर रहा होगा। वह शांतिपूर्वक चर रही हिरणों की पूंछ खींच रहा होगा। मिंकू उन पक्षियों को परेशान कर रहा होगा जो शाखाओं पर आराम कर रहे होंगे। बाकी जानवर मिंकू की शरारतों से परेशान हो रहे होंगे। वहीं, मिंकू हंस रहा होगा और मजे कर रहा होगा, बिना इस बात का एहसास किए कि वह कितना उपद्रव मचा रहा है।

Will be swinging, will be sneaking, will be teasing, will be pulling, will be disturbing, will be getting annoyed, will be laughing

Speak English - 27

Minku Monkey, who is lazy, will be swinging from tree to tree in the forest, looking for some fun. He will be sneaking up on the busy squirrels and stealing their nuts. Minku will be teasing the hardworking ants by scattering their food all over the ground. He will be pulling the tails of the deer while they are grazing peacefully. Minku will be disturbing the birds by shaking the branches they are resting on. The animals will be getting annoyed with Minku's constant mischief. Meanwhile, Minku will be laughing and enjoying himself, not realizing the trouble he's causing.

What will the lion, the elephants, the zebra and birds be doing in the forest in the evening ?

Techo-Ride अगले महीने अपना क्रांतिकारी नया उत्पाद, टाइम मशीन, लॉन्च करने जा रही है। इस कार्यक्रम में, इंजीनियर यह दिखाएंगे कि यह नवाचारी डिवाइस किसी व्यक्ति के अतीत को कैसे उजागर कर सकती है, जबकि मालिक दर्शकों को इसके असाधारण फीचर्स के बारे में बता रहे होंगे, जो इसे संभव बनाते हैं। Techo-Ride यह प्रदर्शित कर रही होगी कि उपयोगकर्ता केवल कुछ क्लिक करके अपने भविष्य की संभावनाओं का अन्वेषण कैसे कर सकेंगे। उपस्थित लोग टाइम मशीन के साथ इंटरैक्ट कर रहे होंगे, अपनी व्यक्तिगत कहानियों को वास्तविक समय में खोज रहे होंगे, और अनुभव कर रहे होंगे कि यह डिवाइस हमारे समय की धारणा को कैसे क्रांतिकारी रूप से बदल रही है। मालिक समझा रहे होंगे कि कैसे टाइम मशीन समय यात्रा को एक वास्तविकता बनाने जा रही है।

Will be launching, will be demonstrating, will be telling, will be showcasing, will be exploring, will be interacting, will be revolutionizing, will be explaining, will be making

Speak English - 28

Techo-Ride will be launching its groundbreaking new product, the Time Machine, next month. At the event, the engineers will be demonstrating how this innovative device can reveal  a person's past, while the owner will be telling the audience about the incredible features that make it possible. Techo-Ride will be showcasing how users will be exploring their future possibilities with just a few clicks. Attendees will be interacting with the Time Machine, discovering their personal histories in real-time, and experiencing firsthand how this device will be revolutionizing our perception of time. The owner will be explaining how the Time Machine will be making time travel a reality.

What will you be doing at this time ten years from now?

जॉय: "जसिका, क्या तुमने कभी सोचा है कि जब हम बूढ़े होंगे, तो हम अपना जीवन कैसे बिता रहे होंगे?"

जसिका: "मुझे लगता है कि हम पुरानी यादों को याद करते हुए काफी समय बिता रहे होंगे, शायद आग के पास बैठकर कॉफी पीते हुए। तुम्हारा क्या ख्याल है?"

जॉय: "मैं कल्पना करता हूँ कि हम लंबी सैर कर रहे होंगे, शांत पलों का आनंद ले रहे होंगे, और अपनी जवानी की कहानियाँ किसी भी सुनने वाले के साथ साझा कर रहे होंगे।"

जसिका: "हम अपनी की हुई सभी मूर्खताओं पर हंस रहे होंगे, और मुझे उम्मीद है कि हम अभी भी नई यादें बना रहे होंगे।"

जॉय: "और हम एक-दूसरे का कठिन समय में साथ दे रहे होंगे, इस बात में सुकून पाते हुए कि हमने पहले ही साथ मिलकर बहुत कुछ सहा है।"

जसिका: "हाँ, हम हर पल को संजो रहे होंगे |

Will be living, will be spending, will be taking, will be sharing, will be laughing, will be making, will be supporting, will be cherishing

Speak English - 29

Joy: "Jassica, do you ever wonder how we'll be living our lives when we're old?"

Jassica: "I think we'll be spending a lot of time reminiscing about the good old days, maybe sitting by the fire with a cup of coffee. What about you?"

Joy: "I imagine we'll be taking long walks, enjoying the quiet moments, and we'll be sharing stories from our youth with anyone who'll listen."

Jassica: "We'll be laughing at all the silly things we did, and I hope we'll still be making new memories.."

Joy: "And we'll be supporting each other through the tough times, finding comfort in knowing we've been through so much together already."

Jassica: "Yes, we'll be cherishing every moment.

Role - play this conversation with your speaking partner.

डॉक्टर: "आपके इलाज के बाद, आप एक बहुत ही स्वस्थ जीवन जी रहे होंगे। हम यह सुनिश्चित करेंगे कि सब कुछ सुचारू रूप से चले।"

मरीज़: "यह सुनकर अच्छा लग रहा है, डॉक्टर। तो, क्या मैं बेहतर महसूस करूंगा और अधिक ऊर्जावान हो जाऊंगा?"

डॉक्टर: "बिल्कुल। आप अपनी ताकत वापस पा रहे होंगे क्योंकि हम आपकी रिकवरी पर कड़ी नज़र रखेंगे।"

मरीज़: "और मेरी दैनिक गतिविधियों का क्या? क्या मैं उन्हें फिर से कर पाऊंगा?"

डॉक्टर: "हाँ, आप धीरे-धीरे अपनी सामान्य दिनचर्या में वापस आ रहे होंगे। हम पूरी प्रक्रिया के दौरान आपके साथ रहेंगे, यह सुनिश्चित करने के लिए कि आप पूरी तरह से ठीक होने के रास्ते पर हैं।"

मरीज़: "धन्यवाद, डॉक्टर। यह जानकर दिल को सुकून मिलता है कि मैं इस सब के बाद फिर से एक स्वस्थ जीवन जी सकूंगा।"

डॉक्टर: "आपका स्वागत है।"

Will be leading, will be making, will be feeling, will be regaining, will be monitoring will be returning, will be living

Doctor: "After your treatment, you'll be leading a much healthier life. We'll be making sure everything goes smoothly."

Patient: "That sounds promising, Doctor. So, I'll be feeling better and more energetic?"

Doctor: "Absolutely. You'll be regaining your strength as we'll be monitoring your recovery closely."

Patient: "And what about my daily activities? Will I be able to get back to them?"

Doctor: "Yes, you'll be returning to your normal routine gradually. We'll be with you throughout the process, making sure you're on the right path to a full recovery."

Patient: "Thank you, Doctor. It's comforting to know that I'll be living a healthy life again after this."

Doctor: "You're welcome."

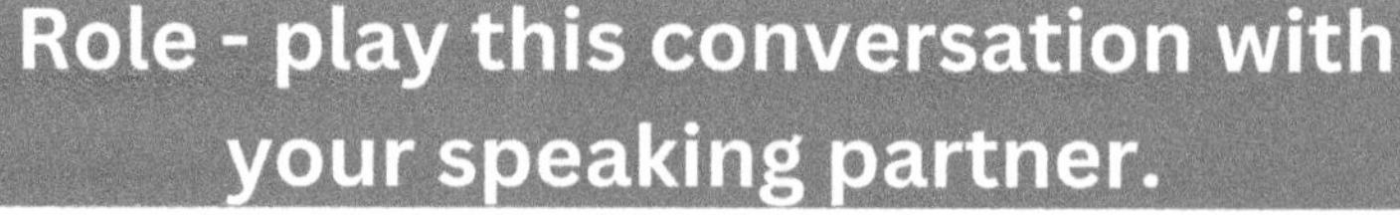

गौरैया: "आज मैं तुम्हारी शाखा पर आराम कर रही हूँ, पेड़। क्या तुम हवा का आनंद ले रहे हो?"

पेड़: "हाँ, मैं हवा के साथ झूम रहा हूँ। कल, मैं और ज्यादा छाया प्रदान करूँगा क्योंकि सूरज तेज़ी से चमक रहा होगा।"

गौरैया: "मैं अब खुशी से चहक रही हूँ। जल्द ही, मैं खाना ढूंढने के लिए उड़ान भरूँगी। क्या तुम मुझे याद करोगे?"

पेड़: "मैं तुम्हारे मीठे गीत अभी सुन रहा हूँ, गौरैया। मैं तुम्हारा इंतजार करूँगा कि तुम वापस आओ और फिर से गाओ।"

गौरैया: "आज मैं तुम्हारी शरण के लिए आभारी हूँ। बाद में, मैं अपने दोस्तों को तुम्हारी मजबूत शाखाओं, ठंडी छाया, और मीठे फलों के बारे में बताऊंगी, जिनका मैं हमेशा आनंद लेती हूँ।"

Resting, enjoying, sawaying, providing, shining, chirping, flying, missing, listening, waiting, enjoy

Speak English - 31

Sparrow: "I am resting on your branch today, Tree. Are you enjoying the breeze?"

Tree: "Yes, I am swaying with the wind. Tomorrow, I will be providing more shade as the sun will be shining bright."

Sparrow: "I am chirping happily now. Soon, I will be flying to find some food. Will you be missing me?"

Tree: "I am listening to your sweet songs now, Sparrow. I will be waiting for you to return and sing again."

Sparrow: "I am grateful for your shelter today. Later, I will tell my friends about your strong branches, cool shade and sweet fruit that I always enjoy."

Describe The Activities

Jassica   Jassica's Mother   Joy

Joe   Tom, Sam, Max

Mia, Ria   Peter

Describe The Activities

1

2

Practice Answering The Questions

- What are you doing these days?
- Are you learning any new skills ?
- What are you thinking right now?
- What are you planning for the weekend?
- Are you working on any projects currently?
- What music are you listening to these days?
- Are you watching any interesting TV shows?
- Where are you spending most of your time these days?
- Are you cooking anything special tonight?
- How are you staying active during the week?
- What topics are you studying in your classes these days?
- Are you reading any good books at the moment?
- Whom are you waiting for?
- Are you making any change to your routine lately?
- What is your father advising you to do?

Practice Answering The Questions

- What was Joy doing when you last saw him?
- Were you having fun at the last party you attended?
- What movie were you watching last weekend?
- Were you playing any games when I called you yesterday?
- What were you eating when your mother caught you?
- Were you listening to music while doing your homework?
- What were you doing when it started raining?
- Were you chatting with anyone special yesterday?
- What were you thinking about during your last trip?
- Were you practicing any hobbies last month?
- What were you wearing during your last birthday celebration?
- Were you exploring any new places last summer?
- What were you doing while waiting for the bus?
- Were you dancing at any events recently?
- What were you daydreaming about last night?

Practice Answering The Questions

- What will you be doing this time next week?
- Will you be studying for your exams tomorrow?
- What will you be wearing to the party next Saturday?
- Will you be watching your favorite show tonight?
- What will your friends be doing right now?
- Where will you be staying in Delhi during the seminar ?
- What will you be cooking for dinner this weekend?
- Will you be traveling anywhere during the holidays?
- What will you be reading this month?
- Will you be exercising in the morning?
- What time will you be leaving for work tomorrow?
- Will you be taking any online classes next month?
- How will Joy be celebrating his success?
- Will you be meeting anyone special this week?
- What will you be doing when the clock strikes midnight on New Year's Eve?

Fill in the blanks with the correct form of the verbs in brackets, using the present simple or present continuous tense.

1. He usually **(read)** the newspaper in the morning, but today he **(watch)** TV.
2. We **(go)** to the gym every day, but right now we (take) a break.
3. She **(work)** as a teacher, but this week she (teach) a special workshop.
4. They **(play)** soccer on Sundays, but today they **(play)** tennis.
5. My brother **(study)** engineering, but he **(prepare)** for a music exam this week.
6. I **(cook)** dinner every evening, but tonight I **(order)** pizza.
7. She **(visit)** her grandparents every month, but this time she **(stay)** with them for a week.
8. He **(drive)** to work every day, but today he **(walk)** because his car is broken.
9. We **(live)** in New York, but this summer we **(stay)** in California.
10. She **(wear)** glasses regularly, but today she **(wear)** contact lenses.
11. I **(write)** in my journal every night, but right now I **(write)** a letter.
12. They **(eat)** breakfast at 7 AM, but today they **(eat)** at 9 AM.
13. The teacher **(explain)** the lesson every day, but today she **(give)** a test.
14. We **(clean)** the house on weekends, but right now we **(decorate)** for a party.
15. He **(work)** in an office, but this month he **(work)** from home.

Fill in the blanks with the correct form of the verbs in brackets, using the past simple or past continuous tense.

1. While I ___ **(study)** for the exam, my friend ___ **(call)** me.
2. She ___ **(cook)** dinner when the phone ___ **(ring)**.
3. They ___ **(play)** soccer when it suddenly ___ **(start)** to rain.
4. I ___ **(watch)** TV when my brother ___ **(come)** home.
5. While we ___ **(walk)** in the park, we ___ **(see)** a beautiful bird.
6. He ___ **(drive)** to work when he ___ **(realize)** he forgot his keys.
7. While the children ___ **(play)** outside, their mother ___ **(prepare)** lunch.
8. She ___ **(read)** a book when she ___ **(hear)** a strange noise.
9. They ___ **(paint)** the house when the power ___ **(go)** out.
10. While I ___ **(wait)** for the bus, it ___ **(start)** to rain.
11. He ___ **(clean)** the car when he ___ **(find)** an old photograph.
12. I ___ **(take)** a shower when the doorbell ___ **(ring)**.
13. While she ___ **(shop)** for groceries, she ___ **(bump)** into an old friend.
14. They ___ **(build)** a sandcastle when the tide ___ **(come)** in.
15. While the students ___ **(write)** their essays, the teacher ___ **(check)** their previous assignments.

Fill in the blanks with the correct form of the verbs in brackets, using the Future simple or Future continuous tense.

1. She _______ **(call)** you later, and she _______ **(be)** working on her project at that time.
2. They _________ **(visit)** us next week, and they _________ **(stay)** at a hotel.
3. I _________ **(finish)** my homework tonight, and I _________ **(be)** watching a movie afterward.
4. We _________ **(meet)** them at the restaurant, and we _________ **(be)** having dinner together.
5. He _________ **(leave)** for New York tomorrow, and he _________ **(be)** traveling by train.
6. You _________ **(receive)** your package by Friday, and you ____ **(be)** waiting at home for it.
7. The teacher _________ **(announce)** the results soon, and the students __ **(be)** waiting eagerly.
8. She _________ **(start)** a new job next month, and she _________ **(be)** learning new skills.
9. They ___ **(move)** to a new house next year, and they _______ **(be)** packing their things soon.
10. I _________ **(buy)** a new phone next week, and I _________ **(be)** comparing different models.
11. We _______ **(attend)** the concert tomorrow, and we _________ **(be)** singing along with the band.
12. He _______ **(complete)** his assignment by tomorrow, and he ____ **(be)** preparing for the presentation.

Answers for Present Tense

1. He usually **reads** the newspaper in the morning, but today he **is watching** TV.
2. We **go** to the gym every day, but right now we **are taking** a break.
3. She **works** as a teacher, but this week she **is teaching** a special workshop.
4. They **play** soccer on Sundays, but today they **are playing** tennis.
5. My brother **studies** engineering, but he **is preparing** for a music exam this week.
6. I **cook** dinner every evening, but tonight I **am ordering** pizza.
7. She **visits** her grandparents every month, but this time she **is staying** with them for a week.
8. He **drives** to work every day, but today he **is walking** because his car is broken.
9. We **live** in New York, but this summer we **are staying** in California.
10. She **wears** glasses regularly, but today she **is wearing** contact lenses.
11. I **write** in my journal every night, but right now I **am writing** a letter.
12. They **eat** breakfast at 7 AM, but today they **are eating** at 9 AM.
13. The teacher **explains** the lesson every day, but today she **is giving** a test.
14. We **clean** the house on weekends, but right now we **are decorating** for a party.
15. He **works** in an office, but this month he **is working** from home.

1. While I **was studying** for the exam, my friend **called** me.
2. She **was cooking** dinner when the phone **rang**.
3. They **were playing** soccer when it suddenly **started** to rain.
4. I **was watching** TV when my brother **came** home.
5. While we **were walking** in the park, we **saw** a beautiful bird.
6. He **was driving** to work when he realized he **forgot** his keys.
7. While the children **were playing** outside, their mother **was preparing** lunch.
8. She **was reading** a book when she **heard** a strange noise.
9. They **were painting** the house when the power **went out**.
10. While I **was waiting** for the bus, it **started** to rain.
11. He **was cleaning** the car when he **found** an old photograph.
12. I **was taking** a shower when the doorbell **rang**.
13. While she **was shopping** for groceries, she **bumped** into an old friend.
14. They **were building** a sandcastle when the tide **came in**.
15. While the students **were writing** their essays, the teacher **was checking** their previous assignments.

1. She **will call** you later, and she **will be working** on her project at that time.
2. They **will visit** us next week, and they **will be staying** at a hotel.
3. I **will finish** my homework tonight, and I **will be watching** a movie afterward.
4. We **will meet** them at the restaurant, and we **will be having** dinner together.
5. He **will leave** for New York tomorrow, and he **will be traveling** by train.
6. You **will receive** your package by Friday, and you **will be waiting** at home for it.
7. The teacher **will announce** the results soon, and the students **will be waiting** eagerly.
8. She **will start** a new job next month, and she **will be learning** new skills.
9. They **will move** to a new house next year, and they **will be packing** their things soon.
10. I **will buy** a new phone next week, and I **will be comparing** different models.
11. We **will attend** the concert tomorrow, and we **will be singing** along with the band.
12. He **will complete** his assignment by tomorrow, and he **will be preparing** for the presentation.

1. A Day in the Life of a Busy Student
Describe what you are currently doing, what you were doing yesterday, and what you will be doing tomorrow.

2. My Favorite Holiday Experience
Talk about what you were doing during your holiday, what you are currently doing to relive the memories, and what you will be doing on your next holiday.

3. The Journey of My Learning a New Skill
Explain what you are learning now, what you were practicing in the past, and what you will be focusing on in the future.

4. Our Environmental Impact
Discuss what people are doing now to harm or help the environment, what they were doing in the past, and what they will be doing in the future to improve it.

5. A Week in My Life
Outline what activities you are doing this week, what you were doing last week, and what you will be doing next week.

6. My Fitness Routine

Describe what exercises you are doing currently, what workouts you were doing before, and what you will be doing to stay fit in the coming months.

7. The Evolution of Technology in Our Lives

Talk about how we are using technology now, how people were using it in the past, and how we will be using it in the future.

8. The Growth of My Favorite Hobby

Share what you are currently doing with your hobby, what you were doing when you started, and what you will be doing to take it to the next level.

9. My Career Goals and Plans

Explain what you are working on now in your career, what you were doing in your previous job or role, and what you will be doing to achieve your future goals.

10. The Impact of Social Media on Society

Discuss how people are interacting on social media now, how they were using it in the past, and how they will be using it in the future.

Practice with Verbs

- A: Arise - Arose - Arisen
- B: Begin - Began - Begun
- C: Choose - Chose - Chosen
- D: Dig - Dug - Dug
- E: Eat - Ate - Eaten
- F: Freeze - Froze - Frozen
- G: Grow - Grew - Grown
- H: Hide - Hid - Hidden
- I: Invest - Invested - Invested
- J: Join - Joined - Joined
- K: Kneel - Knelt - Knelt
- L: Lead - Led - Led
- M: Mislead - Misled - Misled
- N: Neglect - Neglected - Neglected
- O: Overcome- Overcame - Overcome
- P: Prove - Proved - Proven

Practice with Verbs

- Q: Quit - Quit - Quit
- R: Rise - Rose - Risen
- S: See - Saw - Seen
- T: Take - Took - Taken
- U: Understand - Understood - Understood
- V: Verbose - Verbosed - Verbosed
- W: Write - Wrote - Written
- X: Xerox - Xeroxed - Xeroxed
- Y: Yield - Yielded - Yielded
- Z: Zip - Zipped - Zipped

Students,
Practice making sentences with the given verbs. Look around you and notice actions. Try to find verbs for those actions and create sentences. This will not only help you expand your vocabulary but also improve your ability to express yourself in English.
Happy learning!

TENSE CHART

FUTURE

PRESENT

PAST

INDEFINITE

ता है, ती है, ते हैं।
1st verb form
(-) Do not / does not + 1stv
(?) Do/Does + Subject + 1stv
Use of 's' or 'es ' with verb with he, she, it / single subjects

गा, गी, गे।
Will/Shall + 1stv
(-) will/shall not + 1stv
(?) Will/Shall + subject + 1stv
Will/Shall : I & We

आ, ई, ए
2nd Verb
(-) did not + 1stv
(?) Did + Subject + 1stv ?

CONTINUOUS

रहा है। रही है। रहे है।
is, am, are + 1stv + ing
(-) is/am/are + not + 1stv + ing
(?) Is/Am/Are + subject + 1stv

रहा होगा, रही होगी, रहे होगें।
will/shall + be + 1stv+ing
(-) will/shall not be +1stv+ing
(?) Will/Shall + subject + be + 1stv+ing

रहा था रही थी रहे थे।
was/were + 1stv + ing
(-) was/were + not + 1stv + ing
(?) Was/Were + subject + 1stv + ing

PERFECT

चुका है, गया है, दिया है, हुआ है ,जीता है।
Has/Have + 3rdv
(-) has/have + not + 3rdv
(?) Has/Have + subject + 3rdv
Has : He, She, It (Single subjects)
Have : I, You & plural subjects

चुका होगा, गया होगा, दिया होगा, हुआ होगा, जीता होगा।
will/shall + have + 3rdv
(-) will/shall + not have + 3rdv
(?) Will/Shall + subject + have + 3rdv

चुका था, गया था, दिया था, हुआ था, जीता था ।
had + 3rdv
(-) had not + 3rdv
(?) Had + subject + 3rdv

PERFECT CONTINUOUS

Time + रहा है, रही है, रहे है।
has/have + been + 1stv+ing
(-) has/have + not +been + 1stv+ing
(?) has/have + subject + been + 1stv+ing
Use of 'Since' or 'For'

Time + रहा होगा, रही होगी, रहे होगें।
will/shall + have been + 1stv+ing
(-) will/shall not have been + 1stv+ing
(?) Will/Shall + subject + have been + 1stv+ing
Use of 'Since' or 'For'

Time + रहा था, रही थी, रहे थे।
had been + 1stv+ing
(-) had not been + 1stv+ing
(?) Had + subject + been + 1stv+ing
Use of 'Since' or 'For'

Tenses Are My Teacher

Message Of Thanks

Dear Reader, 

Thank you immensely for finishing Volume 4 of "Tenses Are My Teacher." Your dedication to studying these volumes is truly commendable.

I hope, they are aiding you in mastering English fluently, especially in speaking. Your positive response to the book is incredibly motivating and appreciated. Tenses are indeed pivotal in guiding one through the intricacies of English speech.

Continuing with the next volumes will undoubtedly enhance your fluency in English conversation even further. Your feedback on the book is invaluable and eagerly awaited.

I eagerly anticipate your presence in the upcoming volume!

AMRITASHAAN

AUTHOR'S MASTERPIECES

Make Your Notes

Make Your Notes

Make Your Notes

www.ingramcontent.com/pod-product-compliance
Lightning Source LLC
Chambersburg PA
CBHW040802120726
48005CB00012B/1272